THIRTY DIRTY LIES ABOUT OLD

BY
Hugh Downs

ACKNOWLEDGMENTS

Excerpts from Genesis 17 and 21 are from *The New English Bible.* © The Delegates of the Oxford University Press and The Syndics of the Cambridge University Press 1961, 1970. Reprinted by permission.

Excerpt from *The Book of Health,* 3rd ed., compiled and edited by Randolph Lee Clark, M.D., and Russell W. Cumley, Ph.D. © 1973 by Litton Educational Publishing, Inc. Reprinted by permission of Van Nostrand Reinhold Company.

The excerpts on pages 144-145 are from the *Chicago Tribune,* October 6, 1978, page 6. Reprinted, courtesy of the *Chicago Tribune.*

Letter to Dear Abby and the reply, as published in the October 18, 1978, *Chicago Tribune,* reprinted by permission of Abigail Van Buren.

Excerpt from Lin Yutang, *The Importance of Living* (John Day, 1937). Reprinted by permission of Thomas Y. Crowell Company and Curtis Brown, Ltd., London.

Cover design by Gene Tarpey
Illustrations by John Faulkner
Cover Photo by Christopher Little / © 1978 ABC, Inc.

FIRST EDITION

ARGUS COMMUNICATIONS
7440 Natchez Avenue
Niles, Illinois 60648

International Standard Book Number 0-89505-033-1

Library of Congress Number 79-63174

0 9 8 7 6 5 4 3 2 1

To Sadim Young, age eight,
an old man of the next century.

I want to thank Jim Clark, my editor,
for his enormous aid in putting this
book together. He brought to the task
both skill and wisdom, and he isn't
even old.

H.D.

Contents

Prologue 7

#1 An old person is an *old* person . . 11

#2 Old people can't keep track of
family relationships 18

#3 You can't teach an old dog
new tricks 21

#4 You can't do anything about
getting old 27

#5 The "aging" are past their prime . 31

#6 Older people stand little chance
in a country that accents youth . . 38

#7 Older people want to be young . . 52

#8 When you get old you won't
feel good 56

#9 Old age is an illness 61

#10 Arthritis is a disease of old people . 65

#11 When I get old I'll be deaf 67

#12 Old people have no interest in sex . 69

#13 You won't live long if your
parents didn't 80

#14 Thinking slows up as you age . . . 83

#15 Intelligence declines with age . . . 87

#16 People beyond sixty (or seventy)
are too old to have a pilot's license
(or a driver's, a beautician's,
you-name-it license) 91

#17 If you're over fifty and out of a job, you might as well give up 95

#18 Old people are more likely to become depressed 106

#19 All old people are wise 110

#20 Old people want to be with people their own age 112

#21 When I get old I'll have to live in an institution 117

#22 Old people are eccentric 120

#23 Time goes faster when you're old . . 122

#24 Retirement will kill you 124

#25 With a Social Security pension to look forward to, no one need worry about income after retirement . . . 129

#26 Old people need less (of everything) 139

#27 Face it: if you're old you're bound to be ripped off 142

#28 It's bad to dwell on the past 150

#29 Old people die because they're old . 153

#30 People are what they are, so it's useless to try to change attitudes toward the older 156

Epilogue 160

Prologue

A Zen master assigns his pupils *koans* (riddles, if you wish) on which they meditate and which, if sufficiently persistent and contemplative, they might eventually solve. "What is the sound of one hand clapping?" "Show me your original face, the one you had before you were born." "Show me the face you had before your parents were born."

The great and durable baseball pitcher Satchel Paige once offered a sort of koan himself when he asked, "How old would you be if you didn't know how old you was?" Satchel Paige didn't know his age, and neither did Jomo Kenyatta, long-time president of Kenya who died, perhaps in his eighties, in August 1978. Old Satch, like Kenyatta, considered the question irrelevant. He just kept on pitching and striking them out over a long career.

And it was Satchel Paige, referring perhaps again to age, who offered this bit of wisdom: "Don't look back; something might be gaining on you."

As all older people know, over the years a number of lies have been trying to gain on them. And rather than look back or not look back, they should stop, turn, confront and refute them.

Some lies are conscious and vicious, employed to suit convenience, express annoyance, or reinforce prejudice. Others are unconscious, widespread, and perhaps well intentioned—but nonetheless devastating—and they fall from the lips of the young and not-so-young alike. Some are silly, and some downright harmful. All should be examined, exposed, and retired. Because regardless of our age, if we hang around long enough, loose lies will victimize all of us.

And so in this book we look at two and a half dozen rampant fallacies about old. They appear in no particular order of seriousness or depth. They have one thing in common, though: a need for rebuttal and, one might hope, destruction.

Let me mention one important item, my keynote. Satchel Paige in his inimitable manner suggested that there

is really no sound or simple definition
of old. I agree. And after considerable
thought, I have concluded that the best
approach to growing older in our culture
is to abandon the idea that there is
something called an "aging problem."
I suggest that we shed the notion
that problems must be age-specific.
Instead, let's concern ourselves with
individuals.

This seems certain: the more we
try to promote the well-being of older
people by isolating them as a group,
the more we tend to reinforce myths and
stereotypes.

And lies.

Kyoto, 1977

LIE #1

An old person is an old person

To say this is to say "A clock is midnight." The concept "person" can't be compressed into and limited by a slice of time. A person must be considered within the whole spectrum of a life, certainly if we are to eliminate the idea of "old people" as foreigners in our midst. Older people, after all, are not isolates. They, through their and their parents' lifetimes, link us to our heritage. Through their children, they tie us to the future.

The club of the older is one that all of us, barring ill fortune, eventually join. "We have met the aged, and they are us," as Jack Ossofsky of the National Council on the Aging has put it. And each year there are more elders.

Owing to an ever-increasing diminution of deaths over births, the proportion of people sixty-five and over rose from less than 2 percent of the population in 1800 to 4 percent a century later—3 million out of 76 million people. Today the "elderly" number 23 million, nearly 11 percent of the population. A conservative estimate places the number at 30 million by 2000, and 45 million, or 14 percent of the total, within a quarter century after that. More liberal estimates set the total at 72 million, or 22 percent of the whole, by 2025.

However you look at it, conservatively or otherwise, our numbers are huge and will continue to swell. The over-sixty-five club welcomes about a thousand new members every day.

You can look at growing older in one of two ways. One might echo, mournfully, the Egyptian philosopher Ptah-hotep, who wrote in about 2500 B.C.: "Old age is the worst of misfortunes that can afflict a man." Or one might say with Stella Francis, president of the Chicago Gray Panthers: "I am old. As soon as you can say that, you're over the hump. It is not a dirty word. I've earned every one of these gray hairs, and I'm not ashamed of them." At the time, in 1978, Ms. Francis was seventy-four.

So "old" is mostly how you view it. An older person is simply one who has lived a long time. In other respects, older people vary as widely individually as the younger.

I have interviewed one candidate for membership in the club to discover how he sees his future—my daughter's son, Sadim Young. At the time we talked, he was eight years old. Sadim will be sixty-seven in the year 2037, the date some experts predict as America's year of zero population growth.

Q. When do you start getting older?
A. Always. Even when you're little, you always get older.

Q. How do you think you will feel when you're fifty years old?
A. Maybe good, maybe bad.

Q. If you don't feel good, do you think it will be because you're fifty?
A. I doubt it.

Q. Maybe because you're sick or hurt?
A. Sure.

Q. Do you think . . .
A. Older people feel good if they take care of themselves.

Q. Do you think when you're older you'll smoke and drink and stay up till all hours of the night?
A. No way.

Q. Why not?
A. I don't think I want to do that even when I'm young.

Q. What age do you think of as *very* old?
A. Well . . . eighty or ninety.

Q. At what age do you cease to be a child?
A. What?

Q. How old will you be when you're no longer a child?
A. About eighteen, I'd say.

Q. What age would you call middle age?
A. Fifties, maybe fifty-five.

Q. When you get to be eighty, in what ways will the world be different?

A. I hope it's not too different.

Q. I mean, do you think buildings will be taller, that cars will go faster? Things like that.

A. I don't know. You can't know.

Q. How about population? Will there be more people—or fewer?

A. Probably about the same.

Q. The same?

A. Yeah.

Q. Do you think older people—fifty, sixty, and so on—will continue their education, go back to college?

A. They could.

Q. Would you do that?

A. Yes. There'll be different things to know. I'll go back to college.

Q. Good.

A. Maybe everybody would stare. An old person in college!

Q. Maybe when you do that—by the time you're an older person—people won't stare. There might be a lot of older students then.

A. Maybe so.

Q. When you're older, will old people look better than now?

A. If old people look better, it will probably be fake.

Q. How do you mean?

A. It won't be natural.

Q. You mean cosmetics—makeup—or surgery? Or . . .

A. Yeah.

Q. Will you enjoy spending time with your grandchildren?

A. I guess so. My palm says I'll be rich.

Q. And that will give you more time with your grandchildren? Did somebody read your palm?

A. Yes, my mom did. And it says I'll have two children.

Q. That's a good number. How many grandchildren will that give you?

A. (puzzled) That doesn't have anything to do with it. My *children* have to have children for me to have grandchildren.

Q. Of course. Do you think you should quit working when you get old?

A. M-mm—maybe. Maybe not.

Q. Should you be allowed to quit, if you want to?

A. Yes.

Q. Would you quit—retire?

A. It depends on whether I like the job. I might get another job I like better.

Q. Okay. Good luck, and thanks.

A. Okay.

Regardless of age, no person should be bounded by the label "child" or "old person." All are simply persons, and they should be viewed in all their dimensions and treated accordingly.

LIE #2

Old people can't keep track of family relationships

Some old people can't. But then, some people—young and old—can't keep track of anything. And among these are people who because of diseased or damaged brains can't remember or think well. We properly call those persons sick or injured, and find them in all age brackets.

18

And there are both young and old parents who, to their children's dismay but eventual resignation, almost invariably call a child by a sibling's name, requiring quiet correction. One mother of five I knew, entirely sound of mind and body, when calling one of them nearly always had to run through the entire list before she hit upon the right name. That amazed me. Perhaps she was perpetually distraught. In any case, her children got used to it. Those within earshot usually waited patiently.

There are, of course, young "absent-minded professors." And it is not unknown for a young person to step blithely off a curb against the light, the mind far away, if the face is not buried in a newspaper.

Naturally, at nearly every family reunion or annual get-together by near-by members of an extended family, there might be an older person having trouble with his or her memory's "who's who." A grandfather or grandmother might not ordinarily assign a grandchild to the wrong son or daughter, unless the family is huge. Perhaps it happens more often with great-grandparents who might have numerous slots to fill with names.

And there's the point. An older family member, in addition to having welcomed many new folks to the tribe, carries in his or her mind many images and recollections of people you never knew. Don't put that person down for an occasional lapse in keeping track of a once- or twice-removed cousin, or when he or she calls a great-grandson by a son's name. And don't sigh and cluck your tongue, either. That lost look he or she might have for a moment may not be confusion; it may reflect a vision of a face known to you only in pictures.

Don't forget, either, that children get mixed up too. Which aunt, which uncle, is which? Who does that cousin belong to? What is a second cousin anyway, and why?

Memory lapse, temporary confusion, momentary preoccupation respect no age limits.

LIE #3

You can't teach an old dog new tricks

Perhaps not. But we're talking about humans, not dogs. There's a difference.

On the other hand, it may be more accurate to say you can't *force* an old dog to learn new tricks. The old dog may have finally realized how silly and undignified it is to sit up and beg or to chase and bring back that lousy stick time after time. It may, at last, feel

21

exploited. And the animal's motivation to experience more of such nonsense might be as dead as its innocence.

Although it is true that a person can more easily master such skills as speaking a foreign language without an accent at a younger, more impressionable age, the saying "you can't teach an old dog new tricks" implies that older people are not educable. Insofar as this reinforces popular myth, it constitutes abuse. Besides, it's wrong.

Motivation is an important element in learning. You can best teach a dog a trick when the animal is hungry. The dog eventually connects proper performance with a reward—food.

The same with humans. They may seem to learn (or "behave") under the threat of punishment. But negative motivation ordinarily is weak. Humans are more strongly motivated to learn if there is some benefit attached to the learning: the carrot is much more efficacious than the stick.

A youngster proudly masters the task of tying his or her own shoelaces. That act pays off in parental praise and greater freedom and control over the environment. A person learns to pick a lock because that skill might prove immensely rewarding in negotiable loot; the possibility of getting caught doesn't rank high on that person's worry list.

Motivation is probably the toughest problem teachers face. Its absence underlies most every discipline problem in school. The outstanding teacher will prod, probe, and search until he or she discovers just what might motivate each individual in the class to learn. It is not the same with all. To one, good marks might equal praise; to another, quiet personal satisfaction; to another, an opportunity to lord it over classmates; to yet another, an additional step toward a distant goal; to still another, the privilege of using the family car.

The need to consider motivation applies to older people too, and here a number of factors not usually present in the young prevail. For all of us, economy demands that once we find an efficient way to perform a task we stick with it. Inertia might play a role, of course, but more important is the question: What's the payoff for learning something new? If we're to change, we really need convincing that change will bear some fruit, for we've much experience on our side. Moreover, older people know that learning entails effort. An older person has traveled learning roads before; he or she is no longer innocent. That person knows well the difficulties and the chance of failure. And even the most strongly motivated must still cut through a clutter of habits and responses that can get in the way of new learning. Frequently much has to be jettisoned before the new can be taken aboard.

But all this has nothing to do with learning *ability* which, laying accident or disease aside, doesn't diminish with advancing age. The fact that in the course of having learned so much an older person has acquired more finely developed techniques for learning than younger people possess might actually enhance that ability. He or she knows how to go about the task.

Examples of older people learning anew are plentiful. Miz Lillian, President Jimmy Carter's mother, at a rather advanced age decided to join the Peace Corps. She learned a new language—plus a number of other things—and went off to India to serve in the Corps for two years.

S. I. Hayakawa, noted semanticist who as president of San Francisco

State in the 1960s earned a reputation as a hard-liner toward student demonstrators, retired from academia in his seventies and sought other employment. He found it as one of California's senators (the "junior" senator).

Grandma Moses is a classic example of one who switched horses. Born Anna Mary Robertson in 1860 into a farming family near Greenwich, New York, she married a farm worker and had ten children by him. Bothered by arthritis, at age seventy-six she gave up embroidering for painting. After her first New York showing in 1940, her primitive style quickly caught on, creating a great demand for her works. Grandma Moses continued to produce until near her death in 1961.

Otherwise obscure grandmothers (more frequently than grandfathers, perhaps because women tend to live longer) who return to college to win that long-sought-after degree continue to make good copy. But possibly this kind of story will soon become ho-hum, for good reason.

A declining birthrate has already left many school buildings idle. College enrollments are scheduled to diminish in the near future. Because of these factors,

plus the continued increase in the older
population, we might well see a flourish-
ing of adult education in coming years.
As more and more "old dogs" give
lie to the myth, perhaps it will at last
fade away.

LIE #4

You can't do anything about getting old

Here's a two-way lie.

From a strictly logical viewpoint, it's a lie because suicide remains an option as long as one has the strength and motivation to end life. Life can become burdensome for several reasons,

27

none of which has anything to do with "getting old."

The statement is a lie also within the context of a faulty—but widespread—concept of "old."

Ruling out suicide, you can do nothing to prevent time's passing, any more than King Canute succeeded with the tide. Tomorrow, inexorably, you will be one day older than you are today. But there are things you can do about feeling, looking, acting, or *being considered uselessly* old.

There are four kinds of aging.

Chronological. If you were born in 1950, you were ten years old in 1960; and if you prevail, you will be ninety in 2040. This is airtight, subject to no alteration, and probably the only valid definition of aging.

Primary physical. Gerontologists recognize certain processes, not locked into a timetable as birthdays are, but sequentially arranged, timed to the human lifespan and roughly the same for everyone. They include a halting of growth-gland activity (somewhere between ages fifteen and twenty), a slowing of reflexes (late teens, early twenties), and a falling off of acuity in number-sequence memory and some other mental activities (around twenty-six to twenty-eight). They also include a gradual drying out of facial tissues (beginning around age thirty), the gradual thinning of spinal discs and loss of eye-lens flexibility (forty to forty-five), and so on. Some of these processes might be retarded, but none can be avoided. And none is fatal, nor need any really affect a person's life and habits much.

Secondary physical. This is primary physical aging that is accelerated by such factors as extraordinary stress, trauma, disease, and environmental elements ranging from smoking to a lousy diet. A person can avoid a great deal of this type of aging by combining common sense with determination.

Social. Here we have a kind of aging clearly discernible in our culture, and it has had some bad effects. It has contributed to forced retirement, financial exploitation, waste of human resources, prejudice, suffering, and dread. *All* of this is avoidable, and all of it may shortly end under pressure from an aroused people awakened from the nightmare and determined to awaken everyone else.

This kind of aging encourages members of society to believe that older people are of no value to the community or to themselves. And older people are asked to believe the myth and play the game. They are expected to "act their age," to deny sexual desires, to remain docile while being ripped off, to acknowledge the superior wisdom of the young, to accept underprivileged status on grounds that they've "had their turn," to be uneducable, unemployable, and unintelligent. They are expected to remain sedately in their rockers, enfeebled but (conveniently, to be hoped) not ill in any costly way, to be dull to any sense of loss, and to fit the stereotypes of "pop," "granny," or "little old lady," along with "codger," "duffer," and "goat"—these usually preceded by the adjective "old." Actually, while not so identified during their youth, old codgers, duffers, and goats were codgers, duffers, and goats at an earlier age; but society labeled them bucks, whippersnappers, and upstarts then.

The time has come for all old whippersnappers to protest. Stereotypes are funny until they are used (as they frequently are) to justify social abuses.

LIE #5

The "aging" are past their prime

Properly speaking, as my grandson Sadim Young noted, the "aging" are all humans now alive—the infant in the stroller, the retired auto worker in his backyard, the five-year-old girl in kindergarten, the ballet star in mid-leap, the college student, the stockbroker, the baby about to be born—all are aging. When we label people beyond a certain calendar age as the aging, and then immediately attach the tag "past prime" to them, we are merely trying to compress them into a group and at the same time say that all people outside that group are somehow *not* aging.

To make the group more recognizable—and manageable—society imposes restrictions and then cites the restrictions as natural so as to justify an attitude. George Bernard Shaw wrote of how Americans consigned blacks to such jobs as shining shoes on grounds that they were inferior, then proved their inferiority by pointing out that they shined shoes. The same sort of circular reasoning applies to "old" and "prime." An old person is beyond his or her prime; a person beyond his or her prime is old.

We consider baseball players on the downward side of the hill at about age thirty; football players peak a little later. But this varies with the individual too, as we all realize, or should at least.

Who knows at what age Satchel Paige hung up his spikes? At age forty Gaylord Perry, pitching for the San Diego Padres, posted a 21-6 record in 1978. This feat won "Old" Perry the 1978 National League Cy Young Award, the oldest pitcher ever so honored. "They kept saying, 'You're too old to do this and that,' but I think I showed them,"

Perry said. "I'm going to dedicate it to people 40 and over."

George Blanda in his mid-forties continued neatly to split goalposts with placekicks. And don't forget that Muhammad Ali at the "ripe old age" of thirty-six won the heavyweight boxing title for an unprecedented third time by defeating the much younger Leon Spinks. Ali may not have been as finely tuned physically as ten years before, but he certainly knew how to employ the many skills he had accumulated over the years.

On the other hand, the brilliant Russian gymnast Olga Korbut seems to have passed her prime at age twenty.

Prime can depend on the field. Like so many other things, it also reflects the individual. Pablo Picasso, spending several hours each day in his studio, and over a lifetime having constantly changed his styles, kept churning out paintings until his death in his nineties. Many critics consider Picasso's last works fully as fine as any he produced along the way.

Another painter, Georgia O'Keeffe, came into her own after moving to New Mexico in 1929 at age forty-two. At last report, now in her nineties, Ms. O'Keeffe is still turning out art reflecting her fascination with the beauty of the arid land in which she chose to live.

In 1943, the Chicago artist Ivan Albright produced the works showing the gradual deterioration of the central character in the movie *The Picture of Dorian Gray.* At eighty-one, Albright was still highly productive, still staging exhibitions.

Oliver Wendell Holmes, Jr., who became "ancient" on the Supreme Court, continued to read Plato to "improve his mind" until his death at age ninety-four. Associate Justice William O. Douglas, rather along in years when he married a girl in her twenties, remained as sharp as ever with his questions from the bench and his opinions until a stroke forced him off the bench in his eighties. And Douglas remained physically active too. Tramping the trails and climbing mountains continued as his favorite pastimes. His young wife said he had more energy than she.

About Margot Fonteyn it has been said: "As she has gotten older, she somehow resiliently grasped at her ability and hung on to the care of her beauty. She offers now, and for all I know, forever, one of the most emotional experiences in dance. She is full of the autumnal glories of maturity that needs no apologies." A critic wrote of Martha Graham at eighty-three: "She is her own best saleswoman for her body philosophy." And of Joan Sutherland: "Her voice sounds stronger and more lush than ever. Her coloratura ability continues like an eighth wonder. She is aging like a fine wine."

Ben Travers at age eighty-nine in 1975 wrote *The Bed before Yesterday,* a smash hit on the London stage. Dame Agatha Christie kept producing best-selling mysteries until her death in her eighties. P. G. Wodehouse lived until age ninety-three. Altogether he published ninety or so books, the last, *Sunset at Blandings,* appearing shortly after his death.

As Maurice Chevalier neared seventy, someone asked him how it felt. Said he: "Well, considering the alternative, it feels wonderful." The list of entertainers and actors who continued to do well in their sixties, seventies, and beyond is long: Fred Astaire, Ethel Barrymore, Ruth Gordon, Bob Hope, Bing Crosby, Perry Como, Jack Benny, and John Wayne, to name a few. George Burns, octogenarian, has insisted: "I *can't* die. I'm *booked!*"

Garson Kanin in his *It Takes a Long Time to Become Young* tells the engaging story about how, when needing an elderly actor to cast in a play, he came across James O'Neil, with whom he had been slightly acquainted at some time in the past.

O'Neil spent only a little time with the script, but he deeply impressed Kanin with his quick and obvious understanding of the play and the role in question. Dispensing with a reading, Kanin hired him. That pleased O'Neil, of course, but he wasn't entirely satisfied. Kanin didn't seem to care to know much about him, especially how old he was. But Kanin finally asked. Ninety-two. He had played his first role in 1888. And, said O'Neil, "I'm still going strong." Kanin could only reply, "You certainly are."

And in the musical world, who could overlook Artur Rubinstein and Vladimir Horowitz? Their exquisite playing certainly shatters any suggestion that they are "past prime."

These people made their marks some time ago and didn't stop. Well along in years, they continue to produce. They derive intense pleasure from their work, from their contributions to the world. Marc Chagall at age ninety said, "Without my work, my life would be idiotic."

And they seem to take life lightly, looking for—and always finding—humor. Some people believe that a strong relationship exists between laughter and longevity and health. Norman Cousins, late of the *Saturday Review* and a well-known practical joker, swears he recovered from a serious illness simply by finding reasons to laugh and have fun. Could be. Certainly it has been said that some people worry themselves to death.

Exceptions? They certainly are exceptional people. But how many others are there like them known only to a few? How many older craftsmen do you know—cobblers, watchmakers, silversmiths, leather workers, cabinet-makers, or other competent, productive people, "still going strong." They're all around us, I would guess, still in their prime.

What is prime? More than anything else, I suspect, it's something in your head—and perhaps in your heart.

So when you see an older person and feel the temptation to remark that he or she is past prime, watch it.

LIE #6

Older people stand little chance in a country that accents youth

Well, never say "never." If history teaches anything, it shows that things change. And the flow is seldom constantly in one direction.

When we consider veneration accorded age, we usually think of China. And Lin Yutang in his *The Importance of Living* summed up the situation well:

In China, the first question a person asks the other on an official call, after asking about his name and surname is, "What is your glorious age?" If the person replies apologetically that he is twenty-three or twenty-eight, the other party generally comforts him by saying that he has still a glorious future, and that one day he may become old. But if the person replies that he is thirty-five or thirty-eight, the other party immediately exclaims with deep respect, "Good luck!"; enthusiasm grows in proportion as the gentleman is able to report a higher and higher age, and if the person is anywhere over fifty, the inquirer immediately drops his voice in humility and respect. . . . People in middle age actually look forward to the time when they can celebrate their fifty-first birthday. . . . The sixty-first is a happier and grander occasion than the fifty-first and the seventy-first is still happier and grander, while a man able to celebrate his eighty-first birthday is actually looked upon as one specially favored by heaven.

As the American population's median age continues to edge upward (it is now about 29.5 years), we may be witnessing a shift in values here, back to an earlier time. People tend to think of the "youth cult" as a twentieth-century, even post-World War II, phenomenon. Actually it goes back much further. A spot of history might be useful here.

Older people enjoyed respect and attention during colonial times in this country. But before sighing for the good old days, note this: there were relatively few older people around then. In 1790, shortly after the Constitution launched a new government, the median age in America was hardly sixteen, and it remained at that point until 1820! Half the population was younger than that. There were a lot of children romping around, and one reason couples produced numerous offspring was that so many of them died. Around 20 percent of those born expired within the first year—from disease, malnutrition, or birth defect. An equal proportion died short of adulthood.

Life expectancy was scarcely thirty years. Few Americans outdistanced the biblical three score and ten. Living until age eighty-four, Ben Franklin proved to be a rare bird in that as in many other respects. So anyone who lived into his or her sixties or seventies was an object of wonder and respect. Older people enjoyed scarcity value—a fact that may have helped shape attitudes toward the old in China too.

There were other reasons for veneration, of course. People accepted as a matter of course that a person shaped good judgment only on the anvil of years. Having lived longer, an older person knew more, was wiser, and therefore more reliable for council than the young. When it came to skill and constancy as well as advice, people tended to prefer "gray heads" to "green."

Religion had something to do with this. People regarded God as old, by definition. Overlooking the fact that Jesus died in his early thirties, people thought of him as ancient too. Works depicting Christ frequently showed him as white-haired.

In New England town meetings, democracy bowed to age. People took seats first with regard to years, second to estate, and third to usefulness.

Anne Bradstreet, the colonies' outstanding lady poet, summed up the mid-seventeenth-century attitude toward age in this fashion:

> And last of all, to act upon this stage:
> Leaning upon his staffe, comes old age.
> Under his arme a Sheafe of wheat he bore,
> A harvest of the best, what needs he more.
> In's other hand a glasse, ev'n almost run,
> This writ about: *This out then I am done.*
> His hoary haires, and grave aspect made way:
> And all gave ear, to what he had to say.

This is not to say that Americans, while respecting age, necessarily loved the elderly, at least not all of them. The Reverend Timothy Cutler of Yale College, for example, lived to be eighty-one, dying in 1765. One person characterized him in his later years as "haughty and overbearing in his manners; and to a stranger, in the pulpit, appeared as a man fraught with pride. He never could win the rising generation, because he found it so difficult to be condescending [meaning then to treat inferiors sympathetically]; nor had he intimates of his own age and flock." One might suspect that the Reverend Cutler displayed these disagreeable traits when young too, but in any event, at an advanced age he commanded attention: "People of every denomination looked upon him with a kind of veneration, and his extensive learning excited esteem and respect where there was nothing to move or hold the affection of the heart."

The historian David Hackett Fischer (on whose *Growing Old in America* I have leaned for much of this bit of history) traces the beginning of change in American attitudes toward the elderly to the War for Independence and the French Revolution. He theorizes that the twin focal points of those events, "equality" and "liberty," had much to do with it.

Equality did not mean evenness of possessions, and it certainly did not apply to blacks, Indians, or women.

But the idea, along with its companion liberty, affected numerous aspects of life. Liberty came to mean not just freedom from oppressive government, but also from the constraints of age's authority and privilege and from institutions the elderly upheld—family and church, for example. (Probably no one needs reminding that those working for political change in America and France were, by our standards, quite young. Thomas Jefferson was thirty-three when he wrote the Declaration of Independence, James Madison but three years older when he became the Father of the Constitution. Robespierre was thirty-six when he went to the guillotine in 1794, five years after the French Revolution began.)

In America the frontier might have had something to do with an increasing emphasis on youth. True, a frontier had existed since the beginning of white settlement here, but not until after the War for Independence did the westward movement become a flood. A number of older people journeyed west, of course; but all things considered, the young seemed better suited to endure the hardships of a start in a new land, just as it had been mostly young people who came to America in the first place. And most people equated the frontier with freedom from the constraint that a more mature and conservative eastern seaboard society imposed.

Interestingly, Fischer had found the ideal of equality extending even to family portraiture. The earlier portraits of that kind coming down from the eighteenth century show the father as central and prominent, positioned on a horizontal plane above other family members. After about 1780, though, the entire family appears on the same level, the father having become, apparently, chief among equals.

The distribution of wealth in a land of seemingly unlimited opportunity seems to have been a factor in change too. Given equal opportunity, a younger as well as an older person could acquire wealth through commerce or land ownership. Increasingly, material success, not age, became the criterion of a person's worth. Seating in the meeting house reflected this. Access to choice seats now depended primarily on wealth. In some cases the best places went to the highest bidder. Moreover, equality of inheritance, rather than stipulating a lion's share to the firstborn son—known as primogeniture—was becoming the norm.

By 1820, as life expectancy moved upward and the median age left sixteen behind, the elderly became more numerous. And perhaps familiarity bred contempt. Henry David Thoreau, who could at times be maddeningly smug, had this to say in *Walden:* "Age is no better, hardly so well, qualified for an instructor as youth, for it has not profitted so much as it has lost. One may almost doubt if the wisest man has learned anything of absolute value by living. Practically, the old have no very important advice to give the young, their experience has been so partial, and their lives have been such miserable failures, for private reasons, as they must believe; and it may be that they have some faith left which belies that experience, and they are only less young than they were." Sounds pretty contemporary, doesn't it? And this attitude stimulated such sayings as: "I never knew a man who lived to be a hundred remarkable for anything else."

During the course of change, the meaning of certain words flipped-flopped. *Gaffer,* for example, had long indicated respect. By 1820 it had become linked to *old,* implying what it does today. *Fogy* had once referred to a wounded war veteran. By 1830 it too had become attached to *old* to form a pejorative phrase. *Old guard* went the same way. Once a title of respect, now it meant "reactionary" and "old hat." Even before the turn of the nineteenth century, *codger* (again usually connected to *old*) had come to have the meaning it bears today.

As words and phrases switched meanings, so new ones casting disapprobation on older people gained currency. *Fuddy-duddy, back number, old goat, old-timer,* and *pop* all date from the early nineteenth century.

Pejoratives referring to women, incidentally, remained pretty much the same. *Hag* had been around for centuries. So had *crone* and *old maid.* They all remained handy tools with which to put older women down.

Owing partly to the antipathy toward the nobility and the upper classes it generated, the French Revolution changed men's fashions. Hairpieces and toupees replaced powdered wigs, and kneebreeches disappeared. But not only was this change meant to have a leveling influence, it also tended to emphasize youth. Stylish men of the early nineteenth century favored tightly trimmed trousers and coats gathered at the waist and puffed out at the shoulders. Not really much new under the sun, is there?

Women's dress during the seventeenth and eighteenth centuries was much the same for young and older, style depending on social class. Not so by the beginning of the nineteenth century. Now styles differed according to age. Although this trend proved of short duration, it did not die completely. Lying dormant, it surfaced again in the 1920s.

And so, as all this indicates, gerontophobia has a longer history in this country than most people realize. Industrialization, urbanization, the rise of technology, and the growing number of those over sixty—creating pressure for systematic retirement—all nurtured it. But these factors were not primary causes; the accent on youth began before they appeared on the scene.

One related phenomenon does belong pretty much to the twentieth century. Urbanization, child labor reform, and the rise of psychology and human development as disciplines in colleges and university, and probably other factors, led to the establishment of a new class in America: adolescence. Formerly, employment on farm or in factory served as a *rite de passage* from childhood to adulthood for most youth, and it was a brief transition. Now the country accepted the abolition of teenage productivity, preferring to set youth aside for a time in junior and senior high schools, many of which appeared in American towns and cities during the late nineteenth and early twentieth centuries. The "youth market," however, did not become really prominent until after World War II. General postwar affluence had much to do with its appearance then.

Despite obeisance to the young, though, Americans over the years developed skepticism regarding youth in politics, which is interesting considering the relative youthfulness of those who made revolutions and the Constitution. That Theodore Roosevelt and John F. Kennedy became president in their early forties seemed remarkable. Many people without flinching accept the possibility that Ronald Reagan might serve as president in his seventies. And while the median age in the House of

Representatives in 1799 was 43.5 years, in 1975 it was 48.5. In the Senate the change was from 45.25 to 52.5 over that same span of years. The age of the person who fills the position of House speakership and that of Senate president pro tempore and places of leadership on powerful congressional committees has seldom dropped below sixty-five.

We find a similar situation on the gubernatorial and mayorality levels. Huey Long won the governorship of Louisiana in 1928 at age thirty-five, and later Harold Stassen that of Minnesota at thirty-one. Hubert Humphrey became mayor of Minneapolis when he was thirty-four. Dennis J. Kucinich at age thirty-one was elected mayor of Cleveland in 1977. That same year, at the same age, Paul R. Soglin won his second term as mayor of Madison, Wisconsin. A little further up the scale, we had Jim Thompson of Illinois and Jerry Brown of California winning first and second gubernatorial terms in their early forties. While these events did not merit "second coming" headlines, the winners' ages in each case were note-worthy, which would seem to indicate that we usually prefer older men—and women too—as governors and mayors.

The "youth cult" seems to have peaked in the 1960s. During that decade, so influential was the accent on youth that elders unabashedly aped their juniors in vocabulary, speech style, interests, dress—you name it. But, inexorably, time passes. Those who refused to trust anyone over thirty eventually reached that age and exceeded it. That alone did much to alter attitudes.

Gerontophilia might never become an American norm. But those of advancing years might take heart. We no longer have scarcity value. Every year there are more of us, and in a democracy political power follows the numbers. Dr. Francis E. Townsend demonstrated the influence of "old folks" way back in the 1930s. The popularity of his scheme to relieve depression woes— a grant of $200 a month to everyone aged sixty or over provided he or she spent it all every thirty days—had much to do with the passage of the Social Security Act of 1935. We might not see bumper stickers reading "Love the Elderly," but the proven ability of older people to organize—represented today by such groups as the Gray Panthers—is bound to give them clout. Unloved maybe, but not ignored.

LIE #7

Older people want to be young

When we examine the wish to be young again, it turns out that not only do some people want to assume once more the physical characteristics of the young, but also to retain the vantage point experience has granted along the way. The real wish is to still be oneself, but under the circumstances surrounding another. Well, you can't have your cake and eat it too.

One element in wishing to be young again lies in the human tendency to filter out of memory the pain and refine and idealize the pleasure of the past. It's the "good old days" syndrome. And while the old days were good in some respects, they also held their miseries. So with youth. It was not on the whole—with respect to most people, at least—as splendid as it tends to seem in retrospect. Those days were something less than halcyon.

Jonathan Swift once wrote: "No wise man ever wished to be younger." And as another person remarked, "I don't want to be young again. If you do it right, once is enough." Healthy attitudes, and I'm sure points of view most older people hold.

Faust was apparently not a wise man for all his learning. He wanted to be younger so badly that he sold his soul to the devil in exchange for a fling with Marguerita. I've always thought the real tragedy of Faust was that he might have made it with Marguerita at his real age had he come on properly.

Shaw believed that youth was wasted on young people. Bob Dylan refers in a song to having been "so much older then—I'm younger than that now."

Sure, some people want to be younger. And some older people appear to *get* younger. They shed the shackles that burdened them in earlier years, increasing in flexibility and growing in the joy of living. Garson Kanin says that his title *It Takes a Long Time to Become Young* came from Picasso's response to the question "Why do your later works have so much more freedom and vigor than your earlier ones?"

And some young people, on the other hand, want to be older, although few if any want to be "old." Most of us, though, possess the attitude "I want to live to be old, but I don't want to be old right now." Healthy. Why skip any part of life?

When I was fifteen I worked one summer in a tire-repair shop, apprenticed to a vulcanizer named Tiefentoller. Tief heard me complain about being too young—too young to have a driver's license, too young to vote, and so on. He got tired of hearing me and one day sat on me, beginning with the question "How old are you?"

I told him fifteen.

"How old do you want to be?"

I picked a ripe old age and told him twenty-five.

"Well," he said, "I'm fifty-five. And maybe I'd like to be thirty-five, but like it or not I'm going in the wrong direction. You're going in the right direction and you have nothing to complain about and I don't ever want to hear you complain again." That shut me up.

Being young is tolerable, even in the grip of compulsive sex drives and uncertainty, because the young don't know anything better, and it's their occupation to be young, with all that entails. But for lucky older people there is more freedom—and less turmoil. And these, like Jonathan Swift's wise man, never wish to be younger.

LIE #8

When you get old you won't feel good

If you feel bad when you get old, it won't be because you're old. How you feel will depend on the shape you're in and what you do.

When I was twenty-five, I felt bad a lot of the time. I'd get a headache behind one eye and if I climbed two flights of stairs I'd feel as though each heartbeat would pound the eye right out of my head. I remembered that when I was fifteen I awoke each morning clear-headed, experienced no headaches, and suffered no shortness of breath upon exertion. Ten years later I was thinking it was the normal adult condition to feel as I did. What I didn't take into account were the facts that I was eating junk food, smoking two packs of cigarettes a day, drinking too much, and sleeping irregularly and inadequately. I figured how I felt was just the way things were. If anyone had told me that after I was fifty I would feel as I did when I was fifteen, I would have laughed (and laughing would have given me a headache).

The fact is after I was fifty I did feel again as I had at fifteen (after shedding certain habits) but with some important differences: I had a greater capacity for enjoying everything (including some activities not usually accessible to fifteen-year-olds), more endurance, a greater sense and command of comfort, and freedom from adolescent turmoil.

We interviewed an eighty-five-year-old on the "Today Show" in the early 1960s. When we asked him how he felt at eighty-five, he said, "I feel *good*. In fact,

I feel like I did when I was thirty-five. As long as I don't *do* what I did when I was thirty-five."

One study of hundreds of centenarians found that 17 percent reported excellent health, 39 percent good, 33 percent fair, and only 9 percent poor or very poor. And to have good health, by definition, is to feel good.

The captain of a fishing boat came aboard my boat, *Delphin,* one July afternoon to help me fix a water pump. I was grateful and offered him a drink after we got cleaned up. He asked if I had rum aboard. I did. He said he'd like a rum and Coke. I hadn't run into anyone who drank rum and Coke since high school, and as I handed it to him I said, "I'm amazed you can drink this stuff. I'd get an awful hangover from all that sugar."

"Yeah, I know," he said. "I'm sick as a dog every morning. No good till noon." And he slugged down his drink. I stared at him. I saw a middle-aged man who apparently didn't have enough sense to extricate himself from his own trap because he just figured that's the way things were.

The point is, whatever your age, you can make yourself feel bad by getting into behavior traps. If you have no bad habits and still feel bad, then something is wrong. Whatever is wrong may or may not be correctable, but it's not normal at any age, or characteristic of any age, to feel bad.

When a person feels bad, it may be that something is wrong physically, or the condition may be of emotional origin. In either case the discomfort or pain is real. A younger person tends to be more sensitive to a given stimulus than an older person, and may find a given situation (illness, injury, and so on) more painful. A younger person is subject to a greater range of disorders than an older one—not only measles and mumps and chicken pox, but certain arthritic and other degenerative diseases too, and these in addition are rougher on the young. An older person may have a form of arthritis, but statistically it is found to afflict people under sixty in more crippling ways than it affects those over sixty-five.

Painful conditions of psychosomatic origin are not as common among the elderly as among the young. Dynamic emotional disorders tend to smooth out with advancing years. You are less apt to "lose your mind" in old age than in middle age or youth. (See Lie #9.)

But here again the conventional wisdom promotes the fallacy that you "can't expect too much at your age," and doctors use the phrase all too often. The only thing you "can't expect" is to live forever. You *can* expect, anytime you run into a condition that makes you feel bad, to have that condition treated. The treatment might or might not work, but feeling bad results from sickness or injury, and sick and injured people are found in every age group.

LIE #9

Old age is an illness

Here the illness has a name: senility. And senility is a fiction.

In saying this I realize that I run the risk of having this whole book seem a denial that people age. There is no doubt that we look and are different at age eighty than at age ten, and we can't deny that we are mortal. But I should like to show that we are imprecise when we use the terms *senile* and *senility* and to suggest that there really is no such thing, save as a derogatory term applied to older people. Alex Comfort in his *A Good Age* points out that senile "is less a diagnosis than a term of abuse—you're senile if you make waves. That indicates only that your brain is still functioning and they haven't washed it for you."

The medical community must indulge me for a moment and not rush to the judgment that I'm attacking an established medical concept. *Senility,* an inexact term, refers to a disease that damages the brain, whether its origin be in cerebral arteriosclerosis or dissolution of brain cells; and while there are brain-damaged children, the damage is unlikely to entail the complex circumstances of chronic brain syndrome which can be considered *almost* age-specific. And the very old are, it is true, more likely than the young to run afoul of this difficulty with the brain.

However, the word *senile* implies the condition of being old, utilizing the same root—*sen,* meaning "old"—as in *senate, senescent, senior,* and so on. And since the condition is a sorry one, the implication is denigrating. It could be justified only if *all* old experienced this condition, and they do not. So we are talking about a disease (or complex of diseases) that older people sometimes encounter, younger people seldom, but certainly a disease and not "oldness," which the words *senile* and *senility* suggest. Therefore there really is no such thing as senility.

Alex Comfort, again in *A Good Age:* "Dementia in old age is neither general nor common, but because it piles up in hospitals it is visible and frightening. Actually it affects only a small proportion of the old."

Less than 1 percent of old people become demented. Among people not yet considered old (the two age groups below sixty-five) the rate is over 3 percent. (See Lie #22.) These statistics would seem to indicate that younger people are more apt to go crazy than older. If *senility* implies crazy behavior, then its applicability to older persons diminishes.

Custodial treatment of the elderly, including dosages of tranquilizers, is often the substitute for genuine therapy, and this aggravates mental confusion. Treatment should be for illness, not age, and it should take into account life-styles as well as pathology.

If you run out of memory, or thinking ability, or proper digestive function, or general comfort for that matter, it is because you have become ill; and becoming ill is no more "normal" in older age than in younger. There is nothing wrong with getting old; the only alternative is dying young. There is always something wrong with getting sick.

Different ages have different and identifiable characteristics. (See Lie #4.) There are changes in the circulatory and glandular systems during the teens, in eye-focusing functions in the forties, and in such things as skin elasticity in more advanced years. Yet any single symptom of so-called senility can be found in the young as well as in the older.

We attach the term *senility* only to people above a certain calendar age. Yet incontinence, eccentricity, brain damage, high blood pressure, glandular imbalances, forgetfulness, loss of interest, anxiety, and grumpiness appear in people of all ages. Senility is a social concept concocted to serve prejudice and justify neglect. Most of us when we use the word don't know what we're talking about.

LIE #10

Arthritis is a disease of old people

Why do I call this a lie when one form of arthritis—osteoarthritis, or degenerative joint disease—attacks more than 50 percent of middle-aged men and women and around 80 percent of the older group? Four reasons:

First, one has to be specific. Not all old people are or will become victims of either osteoarthritis or rheumatoid

65

arthritis. So these cannot be considered necessary conditions of old age.

Second, rheumatoid arthritis is a crippling disease generally affecting the young, with improvement often occurring by age forty.

Third, osteoarthritis is often a result of stress or injury to joints in hands and legs, described by the terms *farmers' knuckles* and *football players' knees*—the result of hard work or rough sports in earlier years. Obesity can also cause it, for excessive weight overworks the joints' bearings. So what you did or what you were when young can have much to do with osteoarthritis. (See Lie #4, secondary physical.)

Fourth, confusing a concomitant with a condition breeds mischief. Arthritis and rheumatism are concomitant with aging. Attaching them as conditions of growing older is as wrong as considering them conditions of infancy.

The real mischief comes from distorting the image of aging. Anything that reinforces the idea that sickness of any kind is synonymous with oldness is a lie.

LIE #11

When I get old I'll be deaf

If all deaf people were old or all old people were deaf, one could not quarrel with this. But deafness is not a characteristic or a true concomitant of age. Yet society takes the attitude that an older person is hard of hearing *because* he or she is old. This seems "natural" and justifies exclusion or avoidance. People on the other hand make allowances and try to help a younger person who is deaf.

For a time two commercials, one for a lemonade and the other for a popcorn, ran on television. Both featured a hard-of-hearing older person as the butt of fun for younger persons who could hear normally. Our society considers poking fun at handicaps a demonstration of bad taste. Yet there was no public outcry against these commercials, though you can imagine the howl and the blizzard of protest mail that would have resulted if the deaf person had been thirty years old or a child. Apparently if you're old, you're supposed to be deaf. Old persons who hear well are considered phenom-enal. They are not. They are normal.

It's hard to find things that apply either universally or exclusively to the old. Certainly deafness does not. The only one I can think of is that old people have more candles on their birth-day cakes than younger ones.

LIE #12

Old people have no interest in sex

If this be true, someone should have tipped off the likes of Strom Thurmond (United States senator from South Carolina), Leopold Stokowski, Charlie Chaplin, William O. Douglas—and who knows how many other lesser knowns—before they made the mistake of plunging into marriage in their older years with younger women, three out of the four above producing children besides.

Running for reelection in 1978, the seventy-five-year-old Thurmond featured his children—ages two, four, five, and seven—at political rallies dressed in T-shirts marked "Vote for My Daddy." His thirty-one-year-old wife helped campaign too.

Stokowski married Gloria Vanderbilt when he was sixty-three and she in her twenties. He had two sons by that marriage, three children from two previous unions. Stokowski lived, and certainly not passively, to be ninety-five, dying in 1977.

Chaplin wed Oona O'Neill in 1943 (over the strong objections of her playwright father) when she was nineteen and he fifty-four. They had seven children. And Chaplin too lived until 1977, dying at age eighty-eight.

The interest another "oldster," pianist Artur Rubinstein, displays in the opposite sex is well known. And ladies always found Pablo Picasso attractive, right up to the end. Who wouldn't be drawn to such a vibrant person?

True, tongues clucked when Chaplin, Douglas, Thurmond, and Stokowski married younger women. December-May marriages are for the storybooks—and even there seem rather distasteful—

not for real life. When nationwide publicity caught up with Wilbur Mills' and Wayne Hayes' peccadillos, perhaps their age as much as their positions as members of the House of Representatives brought public condemnation down on them.

"I tell you, sonny," an eighty-year-old once said to me, "you never really shake the habit."

Going back in history we have Benjamin Franklin, remarkable in many ways and not the least for his unabashed, constant, and freely admitted and displayed interest in sex. He was in his seventies and she in her sixties when he took up with Madame Helvétius in France. And it was Franklin who once advised a young man to marry, or at least associate with, an older woman. Franklin listed numerous reasons, among which her sexual pleasure was not the least important.

William Byrd, wealthy colonial Virginia planter, lived to be seventy. During his sixty-seventh year he recorded in his diary: "I played the fool with Sally, God forgive me." Later: "In the evening I played the fool with Marjorie, God forgive me." No one

knows how many other times Byrd felt
compelled to beg absolution.

Or to trace the matter even further
back, take the case of Abraham, according to biblical history the progenitor of
both the Jewish and Arab peoples, and
his wife Sarah and the slave girl Hagar.
Apparently barren, Sarah urged her
husband, then eighty-six, to have a child
by Hagar. He did, and the child, a son,
became Ishmael. Later the Lord said to
Abraham, as translated in the New
English Bible:

> "I will bless [Sarah] and give you
> a son by her. I will bless her and
> she shall be the mother of nations;
> the kings of many people shall
> spring from her." Abraham threw
> himself down on his face; he
> laughed and said to himself, "Can
> a son be born to a man who is a
> hundred years old? Can Sarah
> bear a son when she is ninety?"
> He said to God, "If only Ishmael
> might live under thy special care!"
> But God replied, "No. Your wife
> Sarah shall bear you a son, and
> you shall call him Isaac." . . .
> The Lord showed favour to
> Sarah as he had promised, and

made good what he had said about
her. She conceived and bore a son
to Abraham for his old age, at the
time which God had appointed.
The son whom Sarah bore to him,
Abraham named Isaac.

Genesis 17:16-19^a; 21:1-3

In the face of recent research and
wide publicity of the fact that older people are interested in sex—and furthermore have a right to be—and that they
indulge in it, this lie's persistence is
astonishing. Older people have the same
range of sexual interests and problems
as younger people. Differences between
young and old are mostly those of
degree, not kind. The major difference
is that an older man ordinarily needs
more time to become fully aroused.

Still, the "dirty old man," the "old
goat" idea seems to remain virulent.
And this attitude fosters such one liners
as this, frequently attributed to Groucho
Marx: "A man is only as old as the woman he feels." Or, from an anonymous
source: "A man is young as long as
he looks." And these anonymous lines:

It's sad for a girl to reach the age
Where men consider her charmless,

But it's worse for a man to attain
   the age
Where girls consider him harmless.

Much of the problem lies in a faulty imperative: it's not so much whether older people are interested in sex; the point is, they *shouldn't* be. Part of this may stem from ambivalent attitudes toward others' sexuality—any other person's. Part of it might come from doubt and defensiveness stirred by possible competition: "That dirty old man shouldn't be running in a field already crowded. He's had his chance. I have enough competition from dirty young men."

In addition, it's sometimes hard for a child to accept the fact that he or she resulted from parents' copulation. In a child's eyes, parents operate on a "higher" plane. Or if the fact is absorbed, then the child surrounds the act with mystery and makes it a divinely directed event free from carnality. Once a child grants the naturalness of parental intercourse and a resultant birth, he or she may still have trouble believing that parents might have sex for any but reproductive purposes.

When dealing with the sexuality of older patients, doctors can be as misguided as anyone else. Dr. Robert Butler tells of a physician who in consultation described the condition of a vigorous sixty-nine-year-old, listing several disorders but neglecting a genital problem—Peyronie's disease—which is rare, but treatable and sometimes self-correcting. The malady causes pain during intercourse. "He's too old for that to matter," the doctor offered as an explanation for ignoring the condition. But it did matter, a great deal, to the patient. The physician apparently read his own prejudice into the situation.

Not all doctors, fortunately, share that tendency, at least with regard to sex. Let me quote from the 1973 edition of *The Book of Health,* edited by Randolph Lee Clark, M.D., and Russell W. Cumley.

> Although there is a gradual decline in sexual capacity after the age of 40, sexual activity is possible to a very advanced age. There is some evidence that moderate sexual activity tends to maintain normal endocrine balance, and that this in turn may inhibit or ameliorate the processes of aging.
>
> Many older people, including those 90 years of age, continue to

enjoy sexual relations. Their ability to do so depends on whether they have led an active, happy sex life and have no physical impairments. Those who are single or have lost a marriage partner tend to withdraw from sexual contact. People who have never adjusted to their sexual roles during the formative years will tend to have problems in old age resulting in a cessation of sexual interest and a rise in ailments of the sex organs.

A recent questionnaire found that 70 percent of married men over 65 engaged in sexual activities. Since only one third of all women in the United States over 65 are married, it is more difficult to assess the effects of age on their sexual activity.

Potency in old age is conditioned by frequency. Or, as one scientist put it, "nonuse, rather than abuse, causes impotency." Abnormal or prurient concern for sexual function usually signals mental distress. Such individuals may benefit from psychiatric or medical help.

Most discussion on the subject of older people and sex seems to concentrate on the male point of view. This may be, as Simone de Beauvoir in her *Coming of Age* suggests, because "biologically women's sexuality is less affected by age than men's." Utilizing a quote from Brantôme, Mlle. Beauvoir points out that male performance requires an erection while a woman "at no matter what age is endowed with as it were a furnace . . . all fire and fuel within." People once believed that menopause marked the end of a woman's sex life—and interest in the act. Research has shot this fallacy down. As Beauvoir says, "There is nothing to prevent her from going on with her sexual activities until the end of her life."

And expressions of female desire have, according to the record, annoyed at least one male. Writing to Abigail Van Buren, "Old-Fashioned Fellow" grumbled:

> I am sick of reading about "dirty old men." How about dirty old women?
>
> I am a retired bachelor of 63, and, take my word for it, a man who isn't in a wheelchair isn't safe alone anywhere.

Last year I went on a cruise for relaxation, and the women wouldn't leave me alone. One woman, who admitted to being 60, propositioned me for afternoon dates, and even late dates! When I told her I was tired, she dropped the key to her room into my pocket and told me to get some rest and pay her a visit.

A 71-year-old widow kept writing me love notes and sending me presents. Even the young ones made passes at me. One gal in her 30s asked me to dance. Then she whispered, "Let's get together, Pops. What are you saving it for—the prom?"

I may be old-fashioned, Abby, but I still think the man should do the asking. Or have times changed that much?

Bless Abby. She replied:

If my mail reflects the times accurately, most men enjoy being pursued. And what's this "dirty old" business? There's nothing "dirty" about a romantic encounter. And nobody's "old" anymore—

they've just been around for a long time.

The root of the problem lies not in the biological but in the social realm. The facts of sexuality in older people are clouded with stereotypes, preconceptions, misconceptions, prejudices, and a great deal of utter nonsense. To many people, still, it just ain't right for older people to have sex, let alone enjoy it.

Enlightenment is long overdue.

LIE #13

You won't live long if your parents didn't

If Winston Churchill, Britain's great World War II prime minister, took this seriously, he must have had some nervous moments. His father, Randolph, died at age forty-five. His mother, the lovely American-born Jenny, lived longer, until age sixty-six. Sir Winston himself, however, died at age ninety-one.

There does appear to be some relationship between heredity and longevity. But heredity might have had nothing to do with your parents or grandparents dying at a relatively young age. Suicide may have been the cause. A half-million Americans died, many of them prematurely, in the great flu pandemic of 1918-1919. Tuberculosis, diptheria, smallpox, and other diseases once carried off many people at a young age (and TB still accounts for about four thousand deaths a year today). Accidents kill thousands every year. Randolph Churchill had syphilis, which may well have contributed to his early death.

While old age seems to run in families, geneticists are still far from puzzling out the connection between genes and longevity. Nor does anyone know for sure just what diet, environment, degree of stress, and so on have to do with length of life. Even given no accidents, communicable diseases, and so forth, predicting longevity would still remain a terribly shaky proposition and quite inexact on the basis of present knowledge.

Surely under no circumstances should you neglect to follow a sensible diet. And certainly if you have a history of a particular problem in the family—early heart attack, for example—take precautions.

If your parents died young for reasons other than accident, suicide, or communicable disease, you might too. If they lived to a ripe age, so might you. But it's wise to make no bets either way.

LIE #14

Thinking slows up as you age

Brain activity can slow up for a number of reasons: inadequate blood supply, a variety of diseases, lesions, the loss of cells. But cell loss is natural and even at the normal rate of 100,000 or so a day, it's no matter for concern. At thirty or at seventy your loss will be about the

83

same every twenty-four hours. At this rate a brain would last more than 550 years, far beyond the need of anyone save Mel Brooks' Two-Thousand-Year-Old Man. The daily loss represents one-half of one-thousandth of one percent of a whole brain. Insignificant.

But the brain does tend to "melt" away; brain cells, unlike others in the body, are not replaceable. Why, then, can you think better now than you did fifteen years ago? Maybe not everyone does, but accumulated knowledge and wisdom, coupled with well-honed techniques of thinking, often enhance brain activity with age and more than offset the steady loss of cells. Since thinking is a skill and not simply a matter of the number of cells in a brain, organized thinking processes are the key to efficient brain activity. And it is well known that even the brightest, best-organized minds don't integrate more than a fraction of their cells into patterns of efficient thinking. So with 15 to 20 billion brain cells in our skull at birth, we can afford the loss of 100,000 a day without "losing our minds."

The appearance of slowed-down thinking in older persons can come from other reasons than the slight decline in the speed of the brain's computer function, which sets in at about age twenty-seven and accounts for a change measured only in microseconds. (See Lie #4.) And actually, this slowing is discernible mainly in such functions as physical reflexes and reaction time. It is not significant in matters of deliberation or in what we commonly call "thinking."

One reason an older person may appear slower in thought processes is that when you ask for an opinion, he or she must sift through a large store of experience and data before giving you a best answer. A young person doesn't possess such a wide base on which to operate, and consequently might come up with an answer more quickly. And in terms of the time invested waiting for an answer, you probably get what you pay for.

If your brain has shrunk, say, 18 percent by the time you're ninety, but you've moved from using 10 percent of it at age thirty to 20 percent at ninety, you're way ahead of the game, provided you've remained free from injury or disease. The point is that brain activity need not slow up or become less efficient because of age.

Should ordinary thinking activity slow down or go haywire, it is owing to disease or disorder and not to age. There are too many very bright, very old people around to allow the myth that aging brings a decline in thinking ability to stand.

LIE #15

Intelligence declines with age

This, of course, is related to Lie #14. And if you believe that a deaf person is stupid or that a blind person should watch where he's going, or that high blood pressure crops up only among older people, then you may subscribe to this lie.

All evidence—contrary to the opinions of early intelligence testers—

indicates that if health holds up, there is no decline in intelligence with age.

The human brain does shrink as time passes, as we mentioned above. Too bad the brain isn't made up of fat cells, which can increase as time goes on—as we all to our sorrow know. But we also know that few people live long enough to lose as much as 20 percent of their total brain cells, and that it is doubtful that anyone has ever made use of as much as 20 percent of available brain power over a long lifetime. These figures admittedly represent a somewhat simplistic—though I don't think simple-minded —view of brain use and brain loss, but barring disease and injury, the loss is not great enough to affect intelligence.

From a computer-efficiency stand-point, the brain peaks—apparently— in a person's late twenties. Speed of memorization and calculation then declines slowly with each passing year. But no one can tell where intelligence leaves off and the *skill* of solving problems, developed over years of living, takes over. An ability to memorize quickly is a mark of intelligence. But everyone also relies on tricks honed on the whetstone of experience, the older more than the younger by definition. The actor learns ways of memorizing lines faster, the accountant finds or develops methods to improve accuracy and speed, the businessman builds techniques for trend evaluation and decision making based on broad experience. An ability to organize outstrips any decline in brain speed, although many people might take the latter as an indication of loss in intelligence.

As everyone knows, anyway, we have yet to come up with an acceptable definition of intelligence. An ability to solve problems? A potential to solve problems? A potential to learn? A display of one's understanding of the dominant culture? A product of environment, or of heredity, or both? All of the above? None of the above? Who knows?

Unfortunately, in the hands of some psychologists and school people, the so-called IQ scale becomes a bunch of slots in which to file people for convenience, at as early an age as possible. Intelligence is lots of things probably, and experience is by far the least important factor.

If anything, our intelligence may improve with age, even though older people often don't do well on intelligence tests. One expert contends that these tests are administered "in conformity with the expectations of white, middle-class schoolteachers" and as everyone knows, expectation can have a powerful influence on judgment. In many cases we see what we want to see; truth is what we believe. When older people do poorly on some intelligence tests, it might be because they have trouble taking seriously test material that seems dull, pointless, or silly.

LIE #16

*People beyond sixty
(or seventy) are too old
to have a pilot's license
(or a driver's,
a beautician's,
you-name-it license)*

Speaking of silly, it seems that some people believe that certain other people shouldn't fly in airplanes even as passengers simply because they are old.

Maybe the idea is left over from the time when flying meant open-cockpit planes. Not that this makes any sense either. My father, who has been flying on commercial airlines for years, took his first ride in an open-cockpit plane when he was seventy-seven, and he briefly handled the controls aloft too.

In any case, almost no one need be barred from flying as a passenger for medical reasons. If flying were really stressful, airplanes would not be used as ambulances.

As to piloting an airplane, many people over eighty are licensed pilots in powered craft and gliders. Federal Aeronautic Authority regulations reflect a commendable attitude toward the older. The FAA doesn't discriminate on account of age with respect to pilots' licenses. To fly alone or be pilot in command, however, in addition to the proper license you must have a current medical certificate indicating that you've passed a physical examination during the past two years, one year, or six months, depending on the type of license you hold. If you fail this examination at thirty or at sixty, either way you're grounded. If you pass it at eighty, you are, you might say, free as a bird. You can pilot anything you're rated for.

The examinations are neither stringent nor detailed. They simply screen out such risks as people with high blood pressure, those who might be prone to stroke or heart attack, or those with poor and uncorrectable eyesight, inadequate hearing, sluggish reaction time, and so on. Youngsters, too, can fall by the way on these items.

In 1976 the National Aeronautic and Space Administration considered putting an age limit of sixty-five on participants in shuttle flights into space. But the agency decided not to. If the prospective space voyager qualifies and passes a simple physical, age will be no barrier.

As to drivers' licenses, there is from time to time in one or another state agitation to "do something" about "oldsters" behind the wheel. Frequently the "something" means strict and stringent reexamination to test fitness to drive, with the aim of weeding out older people. No one can quarrel with periodic reexamination, provided it's applied impartially to all age groups. As we know, reflexes tend to slow down a bit with age, and younger drivers on the whole react more quickly. Unfortunately, though, accidents are not so much related to ability to drive as to such factors as frustration, carelessness and recklessness, anger, and drinking. Older people tend to be calmer at the wheel. They also exhibit better judgment and less tendency toward recklessness.

Granting a license of any kind is predicated on demonstrated ability and past performance. Age, by itself, should not be a factor.

LIE #17

If you're over fifty and out of a job, you might as well give up

However you look at it, being unemployed is no great thrill, especially if you've been fired—or, to use euphemisms, "let go" or "terminated" (with or without prejudice). Take this case, one among thousands.

"It was the usual kind of day,
ordinary because I looked forward
to it, as I had any other since I'd
been with the company, beginning
in my early twenties. There were
things to consider, decisions to
make, the kinds of things I like to
do and I'm good at. I identified with
the company, and over the years
people saw the company in me.
I'd gone up, not to the top, but close.
No one's life could have been better
than mine, until that day, there it
was. My boss called me in and told
me I was through. The reason?
It hardly matters. If a company
wants to get rid of a person, reasons
fall out of the sky like snowflakes
on a winter day.

"Sure a person sees signs, or
what he thinks are signs. He
thinks, 'Well, I'd better cover my
ass.' But then he also thinks, 'Why
be paranoid? I've been with this
company for years. I'm a proven
asset. Maybe someone, but not me!'
Famous last words.

"He told me I could take a little
time clearing out. Stick around, he
said, use an office and a phone to
begin to make contacts.

"A mistake. Don't hang around. Why? Because if you do you'll be lonely, which just increases your misery. People avoid you. You're a pariah. You got the smell of the pit about you. You can't even scare up a lunch companion.

"But another thing is even worse. When I looked in the mirror the next morning I saw a face I'd never glimpsed before. A defeated man. A worthless creature. An incompetent who must not have deserved the job he had had for years in the first place. I was low, really low.

"I'd always liked a few drinks now and then. But now I discovered that drinks in the past had simply increased the natural high I took to them. They sure didn't help now. They were real downers.

"It was rough. My wife and kids were great, though, and they supported me all the way. I probably wouldn't have made it without them. My wife especially. She pumped up my ego, my morale, forced me to stay in shape, to write a resume, to make calls and send out letters. I finally found another job, a good one.

"But believe me, it's tough when you're out of a job, and especially when you're past fifty."

Some tough, hard-fisted executives have gone on record to support the "traditional" business point of view: if you don't cut the mustard, you deserve to be fired. Businesses are not charitable institutions. They can't afford to mollycoddle or shed tears. And so on.

The trouble is, lack of competence is seldom a reason for firing a person who is past fifty. Most people, at least, are more competent then than when they joined a company in their twenties, or after five years' experience. If incompetency were truly a reason in most cases, one must doubt the competency of a management that hired a person in the first place.

More often, firing can be laid to merger, acquisition, budget cuts, office politics, or new "broom-sweeping" management determined to make a mark.

Interestingly, some companies, stung by occasional adverse publicity about letting people go before retirement but after long service, have taken a new tack. They have set up a service to help such people find other jobs. Typically, personnel people have invented an awkward term to describe it: *out-placement*.

Unfortunately, the pressures and attitudes that work against hiring older people persist. Companies retire employees according to calendar age. Consequently, ignoring the important factor of experience, many employers believe there's insufficient return on investment in hiring an older person who will be with a company a relatively short time. Training a person for a job represents an additional investment, and here we run into the idea—frequently unfounded in fact—that any younger person is more "trainable" than an older person. Salaries tend to be lower for young employees, costing a company less in wages, and executives believe that the younger are more up on latest technology, which of course may or may not be true. That depends entirely on the individual. Periods of high unemployment lend their own dire aspects to the situation: why hire older people when there is a large pool of younger individuals available?

Much of the trouble, as one personnel manager put it, actually stems from simple (or perhaps not so simple) prejudice: "Somehow personnel men and bosses have gotten it into their heads that a man of forty or fifty is over the hill. They think he's physically unfit, can't learn new ways, can't adjust to a new situation. His vigor, his creativity, his imagination are supposedly suddenly nonexistent." And prejudice of any kind is difficult to eradicate.

Some corporations have begun to realize the value of experience. Carl Menk, president of Boyden Associates, Inc., an executive-recruiting agency, said in 1977: "The number of companies interested in someone over fifty for a particular slot has increased 11 percent in the past three years." Some observers think that the trend toward older executives returning to power could become significant in the years ahead. The older, more experienced are by definition seasoned, less likely to be led astray by fad or whim. They tend to be calmer and more resilient in the face of marketing and economic uncertainties than younger counterparts. David Wallace, chairman and president of the Bangor Punta Corporation, has said: "The problems of American business are making decisions more and more expensive. So we need the best expertise we can get and those people whose mental processes help them produce judgments."

According to recent research the *New York Post* reported on January 27, 1977, there is a positive correlation between productivity in industry and worker age. There is also a 20 percent better absentee record among older workers than among younger, and the older experience fewer injuries, both disabling and otherwise.

Relative to absenteeism and productivity, as well as to the general point of utilizing older persons, the story of Fertl, Inc., a small company in South Norwalk, Connecticut, is instructive. Garson Kanin tells about it in his *It Takes a Long Time to Become Young*.

Fertl began back in the 1950s when Hoyt Catlin, during a trip to England, noticed small starter cubes for sale in hardware stores. The cubes, ideal for gardeners impatient for the growing season, contained potting soil, nutrients, seeds, and moisture retainers. Playing a hunch, Catlin in 1954 imported a few, advertised them in magazines and newspapers, and by the end of that year had sold a hundred thousand. He did as well the following year. Then his source dried up: the company went out of business. So Catlin began manufacturing himself. At first he did everything alone. But by 1978 he employed sixteen people, and his gross over the years climbed steadily from $18,000 to $600,000.

Catlin hires older people. He himself, in 1978, was eighty-seven. He had begun his business at an age when most people retire—or are forced to. Most of his workers are in their sixties, some in their seventies. The next oldest to Catlin in 1978 was a woman eighty-three. The average Fertl, Inc., employee age then came to seventy-one. Absenteeism is practically nil. Productivity is high. Employee turnover is so slight as to be scarcely noticeable. The people love their work and Fertl ranks high in efficiency among small businesses in the country.

There aren't many companies like Fertl, Inc., unfortunately. But there do exist today numerous organizations dedicated wholly or in part to helping older people find jobs. Forty Plus is one.

Forty Plus is probably the only organization whose ultimate goal is to go out of business, an objective unlikely to be realized. Interestingly too, the first Forty Plus club formed in 1939, in

Boston, when specific concern for the middle-aged unemployed was hardly a national priority.

The organization is selective, gearing its services to middle-management executives whose incomes have been $17,000 a year or better. But considering the annual casualties on that working level, there are plenty of people in need of help; and in these inflationary times a $17,000 barrier is not formidable.

Members pay a small fee to join and monthly dues, and agree to devote two days a week in the offices to receiving and making calls, handling correspondence, and so on. It's all voluntary, self-help and help-others. Each club—and there are clubs in a dozen such major cities as Chicago, New York, Houston, Denver, and Oakland, plus one in Canada—has a director and such committees as marketing, placement, job counseling, and public relations. Each club also has an outside board of directors, selected annually, to sign checks and otherwise lend continuity.

Each Forty Plus club publicizes itself through newspaper feature stories and television and radio spots. Each develops and cultivates metropolitan business and industrial personnel people. A "management personnel register," in which members advertise their skills and talents through short resumes, goes out to personnel offices every two months. And each club publishes a monthly newsletter for members.

Depending mainly on dues and membership fees, budgets are skimpy, in some instances hardly $50,000 a year. These are too small to pay salaries, but high enough to keep job-finding machinery going.

Misery may hanker after company, but membership in Forty Plus builds morale and dispels the shabby feeling of being unwanted that unemployment generates. Contrary to the case with other organizations, turnover in person- nel keeps Forty Plus clubs thriving. Hardly a week passes in which three, six, sometimes ten men and women find new jobs. Their success conveys optimism to others. And lest someone conclude that these organizations are only for the "young," let me add that slightly more than half the membership at any given time is beyond fifty.

We have, during the past several years, become conscious of the need to stop wasting resources. And one of the resources we must surely stop squandering is the range of abilities older people possess. Not just at the executive level, either, but at all levels. So hooray for Forty Plus and kindred groups.

LIE #18

Old people are more likely to become depressed

This statement, first of all, does violence to the language with its dangling comparative—more likely than what? than they were at an earlier time? than people of different age? It also becomes a self-fulfilling prophesy.

All things considered, of course, growing old in our culture can be a depressing experience. But actually, while depression might be a concomitant of age, age in itself doesn't cause it.

A severe reverse such as the loss of a loved one can cause depression, which if it persists becomes an illness not to be confused with the normal injury that loss brings. Depression amplifies grief to the point of disabling the victim. And this can happen at any age.

Social pressures such as discrimination, lack of privilege, prolonged insecurity, and several other conditions too often imposed on older people make depression among them especially dreadful. But these pressures can be a factor in the onset of depression among younger people.

Chemical changes in the brain can cause depression, and in all cases depression appears to be linked to chemical change. The longer one has been alive, the more likely changes are to occur. But if change brings depression, it creates a diseased condition, and that condition is not a necessary property of being old.

Contrary to popular belief, acute depression is neither permanent nor

incurable and if the victim escapes
suicide, recovery—even without help—
is more likely than not. Financial
insecurity and nonsupportive social
attitudes that foster loss of self-esteem
and loneliness compound the problem
among older people.

Treatment of the elderly often
suffers too. All too frequently the
humane course of thorough diagnosis
and treatment falls by the way in favor
of shortcut pacification by means of
tranquilizers and antidepressants.
Dr. Robert Butler has pointed out that
institutions dispense these drugs "as
much for the tranquility of the institution as for the comfort of the patient."

Acute depression is a common
cause of suicide among all ages,
although it is far from the only one.
The collapse of the will to live (or placing
the highest value on not staying alive)
appears more frequently among older
white males than among any other
group. The United States Public Health
Service reported in 1968 that suicide
figures for this group ran 18.8 per
100,000 in males under sixty-five and
41.7 per 100,000 in those beyond that
age. Among females the rate was 7.6 per
100,000 in the under-sixty-five group,

dropping to 7.16 per 100,000 in the over-
sixty-five segment.

The why of this incidence of over-
sixty-five male suicide remains
undiscovered. Depression, of course,
is not the culprit in every case. A man
terminally ill, for example, might take
himself out of the way without being
depressed in any chemical sense.

Depression itself, whether it leads
to suicide or not, is certainly not limited
to males or to a particular age group.
It is therefore fallacious to regard the
disorder as a condition of age.

LIE #19

All old people are wise

No more than all old people are "senile" or dotty. Age can bring wisdom, but it doesn't guarantee it by any means.

A young dolt may very well survive to become an old dolt. But in the intervening years that person has had opportunities to learn something, to

develop sound thinking habits, and—
maybe—to become wise.

While we can't say that most old
people are wise, most wise people are
old—at least they're not very young.
Wisdom is not a gift of the gods, but the
passage of time does lend opportunities
to acquire it.

The difference between conventional wisdom and real wisdom—if any—
I must leave to philosophers. I think,
though, that most everyone will agree
that whatever wisdom is, not all old
people possess it. So some good things
as well as bad things don't necessarily
go with age.

LIE #20

Old people want to be with people their own age

Fatuous. A sloppy generalization often based on a desire to segregate old people so they'll not be underfoot, a reminder of our own vulnerability, or one found if not implied in real estate advertising.

And what does it mean? Which old people? Different people want different things.

John Jones has friends of all ages and loves children. The outlook of most people her own age annoys, even depresses, Peg Miller. Bill Smith needs people with interests and experiences similar to his own, and he finds them mostly in his own age group. The idea that old people want to be with old people lumps everyone into a group and endows them all with the same characteristics.

It is certainly true that enough older people wish to be with others of their age to make "retirement" or "sunset" communities viable means for profit among real estate developers. Some are rip-offs; others appear to work out to everyone's satisfaction. For those who want and can afford this kind of life and whatever amenities attached, fine. But not everyone does, regardless of wealth, and just because he or she is older, a person doesn't have to be considered a candidate for a retirement community.

People sixty-five and over have one thing in common: they're all beyond sixty-five. And there the universality ends. They do not all like the same things or do the same things, any more than they all look alike.

It is sad that there are older people in this country who very much want to spend time with children and who have little or no opportunity to do so. For those of limited incomes, though, there is an avenue to being both useful and with kids. This is the Foster Grandparent Program.

Now a part of federally supported ACTION—which includes the Peace Corps, Vista, and like groups—a Foster Grandparent Program operates in numerous cities. I quote from an ACTION booklet:

> They are retired Americans, but otherwise a hard group to pin down: low-income men and women between the ages of 60 and 93, from all over the country and from every kind of background. Some are retired nurses or pullman porters, others have worked as cooks, office workers, beauticians, truck drivers, housewives. Now they each put in 20 hours a week with disadvantaged children who also know no common denominator. Many are in hospitals; others meet their Foster Grandparents in correctional institutions or in day care centers. . . .

Foster Grandparents' lives are full of tomorrows: they plan for the futures of the children they serve, and maintain active relationships with other Foster Grandparents, with institution staff, with parents of the children, with their communities. In keeping busy, alert, interested and interesting, they become proof of the adage, "The great use of life is to spend it for something that will outlast it."

Before entering service, Foster Grandparents receive 40 hours of orientation in the specific work they have volunteered to do. They then become an integral part of the child care team of the institution or agency to which they are assigned, working under direct supervision of the staff and attending in-service training sessions held once a month.

The program calls for four hours per day, five days a week, each day divided between two children. Although in the course of their relationships with the children they may assist in physical or speech therapy, change an infant's diapers or help with homework, the emphasis of their assignments is more intimate. Invariably they come quickly to behave as grandparents behave—fighting for their children by insisting on treatment or better shoes, or reading to them, talking, and playing games.

A person has to be below a certain income to qualify as a Foster Grandparent, and this varies according to cost of living state by state. The lowest is $3,140 annually and the highest, in Alaska, is $6,055. And no one will wax rich in the program, at least monetarily. The pay is $1.65 an hour, $1,640 per year.

Right now more than sixteen thousand older people serve as Foster Grandparents. And who benefits more, the older people or the children? Hard to say.

LIE #21

When I get old I'll have to live in an institution

Not necessarily. Doubtful, in fact. Today only one older person in five does. About 80 percent of old people live in their own homes or with relatives. And not everyone admitted to an institution is there against his or her wishes.

Furthermore, a sizeable fraction of homes for the aged are nonprofit, and not all the proprietary (money-making) homes are bad. Recent scandals involving nursing homes have singled out some really horrible examples of abuse and neglect, motivated by greed. And many of these facilities are substandard. Such nursing homes have been characterized as "a facility that has few or no nurses and can hardly qualify as a home." These places are dreadful, and they should be spotlighted and changed or closed.

In the last five years or so steps have been taken to make a clearer distinction between reversible and chronic brain disorders. Now many older people suffering from a combination of over-medication, neglect, and misdiagnosis can be restored to health instead of being cast into custodial environments that only worsen their condition. But progress is slow, even in medical and psychiatric circles, because of stubborn prejudices against the old.

Any of us runs the risk of running out of health and money before running out of time. And we might have no relatives who wish—or are financially able—to provide care when we can't provide it ourselves. Then there remain only those institutions whose business it is to care for such cases, even though many such establishments do not provide adequate, or even humane, care.

But statistics show that, for the randomly chosen individual, the chances of winding up in an institution are relatively slim. With time, and given a continuation of present trends, the chances become even more slender.

LIE #22

Old people are eccentric

Often old people are liberated.
Then, as Garson Kanin and Pablo
Picasso would say, they have become
young—young enough to "do their own
thing."

A twofold implication lies behind
the assertion that old people are eccentric. First, independent or nonconformist behavior is acceptable in the young,
not the old. Second, when older people

behave with disregard for conformity, they are somehow more of a threat, an outrage, or an object of ridicule.

A young eccentric is seen as innovative, a maverick, marching to a different drummer. An old eccentric is said to be in his or her dotage.

Old people who have acquired any wisdom at all are apt to conclude that much "normal" human behavior is unnecessary, or silly, or a waste of time—time that becomes more precious as wisdom brings its full realization of mortality and the importance of not spending what's left of life on gestures of conformity, protocol, and inhibition.

Pianist Paolo Gallico in his late years often interrupted a formal recital to repeat part of a Beethoven sonata for the audience, saying, "Isn't that lovely, right there? I'll play that part for you again." Eccentric? Delightful!

When we see nonconformist behavior that is truly irrational, dangerous, or damaging to the individual or the community, we are dealing with mental disorders, not with age. We all have our peculiarities, none of which are necessarily connected with age or mental disability.

LIE #23

Time goes faster when you're old

Calling this a lie could start an argument. Almost everyone will vouch for the statement, remembering that when a child, each day in school took about a week to unfold, summers were endless, the year a decade. And now time zips by.

The real change is probably that any given period of time appears to have gone by faster when we are older, but only at its end.

A second's a second, an hour's an hour, at age five and fifty. I'm certain these facts undergo no change with respect to a person of eighty. The perceived rate of time may be altered by a few degrees of fever or by a psychedelic drug, or as a consequence of certain types of brain abnormality or damage. But normal consciousness tends to regard the passage of time at a constant, established rate.

Why, then, do days slip by at what seems an accelerated pace when we look back? "Where has the year (decade, week, day) gone?" "Is it Friday (1979, autumn, 5:30 P.M.) already?" "Start *dating?* You're still a child!" Time, as they say, sneaks up on us.

Maybe it's because we consider time in the light of our total sum of conscious memory: a year is 50 percent of a two-year-old's life, 1 percent of a centenarian's.

In the context of previous experience, accumulated units of time, the perspective of memory, we gauge time past on an ever-shrinking scale. But time present doesn't move faster with age, and no one can be cheated of a single moment of his or her life. We tend as we age to make longer-range plans up through midlife.

LIE #24

Retirement will kill you

Maybe, maybe not. Depends pretty much on you. True, retirement seems to drain the life from many people, and in short order. Retired at sixty-five, buried a year later. But this need not be, by any means.

Certainly mandatory retirement according to calendar age might be hard to take, and it can be destructive. Feelings of uselessness, sudden loss of power, inactivity, and boredom can destroy a person of any age, but particularly the older. But retirement need not entail any of these. A person with a sense of security, sound physical and mental health, self-motivation, and multiple interests is surely no candidate for oblivion upon retirement.

Sometimes, it seems, a man's retirement is harder on his wife. As Casey Stengel's wife said when he finally hung up his uniform, in his seventies: "I married him for better or for worse, but *not* for lunch."

It naturally makes more sense to retire *to* something instead of *from* something. Retiring from work can be like being dropped off a cliff. Or it might be like parachuting from a plane toward a target on the ground. In either case it's a bit of a jolt, but there's more of a future in the one attitude than in the other. If you can retire to the farm, to painting, to writing memoirs, to world travel, or to other activities for which time has been lacking in the past, go right to it. Alex Comfort said that in his opinion the ideal time of retirement is about two weeks. The transition period might be longer for some people, shorter for others.

So the upshot is, the sensible person doesn't really retire. He or she changes activities or occupation.

Capacity for real idleness varies greatly among individuals. Some people can endure separation from constructive physical or mental activity for only a few hours at a time—maybe even only a few minutes. Others can go for weeks or years without purposeful action or any planning beyond the next diversion. One person is not necessarily "better" than another in this respect, and most of us fall somewhere between the extremes. The only thing that counts is our attitude toward our condition: if we are happy being busy every moment, or in complete and endless idleness, we certainly are "better" off than if miserable and pressured by activity or bored by inactivity.

The father of a friend of mine has been retired and as of this writing still doing nothing for nearly twenty years. He goes out to meals occasionally and enjoys movies and television and flowers (which a gardener cares for), and he reads. But he possesses no drive to perform constructive work, no passion for hobbies, and no need to be regarded as a "force" of any kind. He says his civil service job was unpleasant, and he couldn't wait to retire. He retired, and he hasn't regretted it.

Inner rather than outer circumstances seem important. Many a person has been urged to "take up a hobby" for relief from work pressures, only to pump the same kind of pressure into it: the golf score must be the lowest, the model trains or stamp collection the finest, and so on. Up to a point this is healthy. But if a person be driven and compulsive, a hobby is no more therapeutic than an occupation under the same circumstances.

On balance, it's better to have a hobby or another skill to occupy oneself than to arrive at retirement with nothing to do, no interests at all save in the job that is no more—at least for you. And certainly if you derive satisfaction from accomplishing, from being respected, needed, and busy—and most of us do—then it's wise to be armed before facing retirement with activities and interests that will enhance your chances of achieving those goals.

Forced retirement can be cruel and destructive, like being turned into a nonperson, like being drummed out of the corps. Yesterday, power and respect, usefulness and satisfaction; today, nothing. This can be traumatic, even with the most careful preparation. And, unfortunately, many people don't prepare. Then things are worse.

Barring illness, the self-employed can choose when and whether to retire. Most of us cannot. It'll be at sixty-five, or now in many cases seventy, but in any case at some point retirement is today. So remember: one who has been retired (a retiree) is a victim. One who retires (a retirer) is still in command, and need suffer no hurt.

Abandonment kills, not retirement.

LIE #25

With a Social Security pension to look forward to, no one need worry about income after retirement

Well, to begin with, it's not a pension. It's insurance. There are some elements of pension planning in Social Security, but the system is one of pooled resources to meet needs—and this is the essence of insurance. In this case it's

129

insurance against total lack of income in old age.

Second, contrary to some opinions, Social Security is not charity. It is no more charity than are dividends paid on investments, or returns from an insurance policy into which you've paid premiums. Whether you get out what you put in depends on the size of your total contribution and how long you live. But Social Security is a just return, not a gift.

Social Security benefits will keep you in your old age? You don't need an ear trumpet to catch millions of experienced Americans yelling "No!"

As we all know, the Social Security System was one response to the Great Depression of the 1930s. Not that it offered any relief right then but, its sponsors hoped, it would provide older people a cushion, however thin, in the future. At the time we had no idea how skimpy that padding would prove to be.

Even so, the idea went down hard in a country that had enshrined free enterprise, self-reliance, and "small" government. The American way was to look ahead and save for your own old age. Anyone who did not was obviously a grasshopper, not an ant, a heedless person deserving little sympathy and surely no "public handouts." Of course, no matter how diligently a worker might lay aside a portion as savings from wages that usually were far from munificent, a period of unemployment or illness could wipe him or her out. And during the early 1930s bank failures, destroying many life's savings, made a mockery of whatever strength of moral fiber putting money aside for the future represented. Today, even with wages considerably higher than then, a spiraling cost of living makes saving for any purpose difficult.

In any event, a congressional majority in the 1930s agreed that some kind of old-age insurance had become imperative. Critics called the Social Security program socialistic—and they certainly were right. Yet it was not entirely so. Social Security was not to be a right, but a benefit, which nudged it toward the capitalistic way. Furthermore, the program would be self-supporting, entirely dependent on contributions from both employees and employers, not at all on general revenues. In effect, a person entered a system of enforced savings. And while Congress originally exempted numerous occupations—

farming, for example—few are left out today. Nearly all of us—the self-employed included—as we say, "pay Social Security."

The Social Security System has its problems, not the least of which is the possibility that, as the population grows older and people live longer, payments to beneficiaries might deplete available funds. This lay behind the congressional decision in 1978 to boost drastically employee-employer contributions beginning in January 1979, after Congress turned down proposals to tap general revenue funds to the extent necessary to bolster the system. In effect, as Social Security rolls swell, younger workers contribute not only to their own retirement, but to that of a growing number of other people as well. In 1947 there were twenty-two workers for each Social Security recipient. Today the ratio is seven to one. By the year 2000 it might be two to one.

Another problem has to do with inflation. Periodic increases in payments, almost as regular during election years as leaves coming down in the fall, have been the rule. But these have not kept pace with the erosion in the dollar's purchasing power.

Then there is the ceiling on the amount of income a Social Security beneficiary can earn without losing a portion of his or her payment. The ceiling doesn't apply to those over seventy-two or to "unearned" income from such items as dividends or rents. Congress has raised the limit from time to time, and eventually it might disappear entirely. In the meantime, people find ways around it. One is to bulk additional income within a short period, such as a quarter of the year, receiving none during the remainder. This increases income and reduces annual Social Security payments only slightly, and the practice is quite legitimate. Another method, not quite so on the up-and-up, is to arrange for extra income to be paid for in cash, usually untraceable.

Still another problem is that, in many cases, income from Social Security for a married retired couple is lower than that for two single individuals. This has led who knows how many retired widows, widowers, and divorced individuals to "live in sin." Tongues may wag, but the out-of-wedlock arrangement for many is economically advantageous.

Under the best of circumstances,

laying aside the well-to-do, as Jack Ossofsky of the National Council on the Aging has said, "There just ain't much gold in those golden years." About one out of every twelve couples and one out of every four retired single or widowed persons rely almost entirely on Social Security. In 1977 about 34 million received monthly benefits, a total of $81.7 billion that year. Twelve million of these were under sixty-five, eligible for disability, widows', orphans', and other benefits besides retirement that are part of the system. The guaranteed minimum benefit in 1977 was $189.40 per month for individuals and $284.10 for couples. So on the whole Social Security replaces from 30 to 46 percent of the average person's working income. This is somewhat less than in other countries, where Social Security is older and where, in many cases, general revenue funds at least supplement the programs.

The replacement proportion amounts to a maximum of 60 to 65 percent in Italy, France, West Germany, Austria, and Sweden. In some Communist countries it is 75 percent, although there, on the other hand, wages are generally lower than elsewhere. (Not that everything is rosy in other countries, of course.

According to the *New York Times,* the state-financed Soviet system replaces from 50 to 55 percent of income, Social Security payments are low, and increases are unheard of.)

One can cite many Social Security horror stories, meager benefits forming the nucleus of the plots. One couple in the Chicago area, for example, got along quite well on his income, supplemented in later years from hers as a civil servant, raising and educating three children. Then emphysema forced him into early retirement and a few years later he died. He had received Social Security disability but no company benefits. His widow retired at sixty-five, falling a number of months short of qualifying for a civil service pension, on $69.23 a week from Social Security. Her rent for a one-bedroom apartment ran $39.23 a week, and medical expenses to care for her diabetes ate up much of the remainder. One winter the gas company cut off her supply because she couldn't pay a $30 bill. "The Social Security doesn't keep up with the costs at all," she said. "You work real hard all your life, earn a lot of money and pay a lot of taxes, and you get nothing out of it." And this is no atypical case.

Civil servants under pension plans fare somewhat better, and the number of people covered by federal plans alone totaled 2.5 million in 1976. As a rule, public pension plans provide regular increases to match those in the cost of living. Local civil service pension systems can get into trouble though. Unfunded liabilities of $6 billion saddled the New York City firemen's pension plan in the mid-1970s, contributing to that city's financial plight at the time. As someone said, "The firemen are not dying when they are supposed to." And no wonder: the plan was based on life expectancy tables of 1941.

Persons covered by both Social Security and private pension plans are best off, although we've learned in recent years that many company plans are shaky at best. Double coverage applies to relatively few workers, and moreover, total income from benefits from both sources averages about 56 percent of replacement of preretirement income.

One thing is certain: most people upon retirement face the need to make do on half or less than half the income they've been used to. This is a bare, bleak fact of life in America today.

The problem is a tough one.
James H. Schulz of Brandeis University, an expert on the economics of aging, has argued that "We should expand Social Security moderately and get the replacement rate up to 55 percent for the average worker. Then he will not have to worry if he is not covered by a pension plan or is covered by one that is bad." This would seem a modest goal, but even were it achieved, inflation could wipe out any gain.

For more and more people every year, Social Security becomes the only means of income, and for millions it is insufficient to meet just everyday needs. The huge increase in contributions effective in 1979 might not stick, for numerous reasons. Then what? The alternative might be finally to draw on general revenues. The question then becomes: Will the citizens of the richest nation on earth agree that they can afford it?

In the 1960s the average ratio of Social Security expenditures to gross national product for thirty industrialized countries was about 14 percent. The Scandinavian countries averaged 12 to 13 percent, Canada 9.9, and Great Britain 6.7. At 4.2 percent the United

States squeezed in barely above Portugal. None of the systems is ideal; ours lags far behind adequacy.

Who are we cheating? Today's elderly, certainly. But all the rest of us too. And the oncoming old will be worse off than today's because they will have more years of retirement to provide for.

By ignoring the problems, by failing to muster the will to pay the cost of bringing meaningful reform to the Social Security System is to walk blindfolded off a cliff.

ANNUAL BUDGET

1/5 EYE EXAM.
1/2 PAIR OF GLASSES
7% of TOP COAT.
1 1/4 DRESS
1% OF SOFA.
$91.00 TRAVEL, HOBBIES

LIE #26

Old people need less (of everything)

Sure, maybe it's only a couple now, the kids all moved away. Sure, maybe the mortgage's paid. And sure, most older people don't spend wildly on nights on the town.

Yet even after adjustment for these and other items, many older people have inadequate resources. But we expect them to be satisfied because "experts" in and out of government estimate what older people need and erect guidelines we cheerfully accept. The trouble is, estimated budgets for the old reflect not what they need so much as what they spend. Here again we have a tautology: older people must need less because they spend less.

Older people spend less, certainly, but mainly because they have less to spend.

The myths of diminished needs, of adequate Social Security, that old people's dreams, tastes, expectations somehow shrink and even atrophy—all these promote the idea that the elderly are not an appropriate matter for concern or financial parity because their needs are fewer. We assume that older people are less interested than those of other age groups in appearance, recreation, pleasant home environments, and even, in some cases, food. Older people can be above the poverty line and within the "modest but adequate" Bureau of Labor Statistics intermediate budget figures and still be in many ways impoverished.

For the retired couple in 1971, BLS figures allowed such items as one-fifth of an eye examination per year per person, one-half pair of glasses, 7 percent of a

man's topcoat, and one and a fourth
street dresses for a woman. They then
went on to grant 1 percent of a sofa each
year and $91 for both for travel, hobbies,
and miscellaneous leisure expenses.
Now, with respect to total allowance for
men's clothing per year, contrast these
"adequate" BLS figures: $94 for the
retired person, $204 for the younger
working man. Those who played with
the figures apparently assumed that
retired people naturally lead inactive,
drab lives. Well, if they stuck with those
figures, they'd have to.

Why, one might ask, should
"adequacy" and "poverty-line" points be
so drastically different for older and
younger? Whatever the figures experts
arrive at, too high or too low, why such
wild distinctions based on age?

Let's agree that on the whole older
people need less than younger ones.
But let us also demolish the idea that
what older people spend is any criterion
of their need. And let's face the fact that
millions of older people have inadequate
resources to provide for needs much
less a little pleasure. We might even go
so far as to ask older people about the
matter, rather than rely on the almost
playful figures statisticians juggle.

LIE #27

Face it: if you're old you're bound to be ripped off

Well, let's face this at least: if you're old you're likely to have many opportunities.

To call them wolves would be to insult *canis lupus,* whose social sense in many respects outshines that of humans'. But those who prey on older people, and there are plenty of them, are predators of the worst kind.

I'm not talking about mugging. This is indeed a serious problem and many older people justifiably live in fear of it. But mugging is a more random event, not to be classified with sales efforts deliberately designed and coolly executed to separate older people from their money.

Those who run shoddy proprietary "retirement" or "rest" homes fall into this category. So do unscrupulous real estate promoters, insurance agents, and home heating and repair operators. All these view the elderly as easy marks.

Fraudulent—or at least slippery—land schemers may go back to near the time that humans first began to live in settled communities—about eight thousand years ago—when, perhaps, a desire to own real estate first became a part of "human nature." Who knows what slick land deals might have been a part of ancient Mesopotamian life? One can imagine wily land speculators unloading tracts along the Tigris and the Euphrates, touting plots offering splendid "river views" that became distressingly apparent during the flooding season.

Whenever the whole thing began, little has changed. The scene in the southwest and in parts of Florida for many people remains the same. Fond visions and expectations soon lie inundated, or erode under the pounding of wind-whipped desert sand. If anything is different, it's that during recent years the pitch has been increasingly toward the elderly.

Take one glittering proposition in Arizona. Said one rueful woman of sixty-six, who moved there with her husband expecting comfortable retirement: "When we got here, we saw how so many of the lots flooded out. We saw one family watch as their trailer sank into the creek as it swelled." (Yes, it does rain occasionally in Arizona, sometimes with devastating results.) The couple had paid $3,500 for their land. "I haven't sold it so far," the woman went on, "because I wouldn't want to sell someone a piece of property the way [the company] did." At this writing the founder of the company, which paid $200 for lots it unloaded for from $3,000 to $4,000, sits out a prison sentence.

Another couple bought a lot in New Mexico and built a $27,000 retirement home on it. Well, as the gentleman said, "If they followed through on those claims of a shopping center, hospital, a regular community in itself, the place could still take off like a skyrocket." But, he continued, "It's been a disaster. Right now, who the hell wants to buy out there? We rented the place for awhile, but for the last year and a half there's been no one living there. That damn lot isn't worth $100."

Developers frequently paint glowing pictures of communities blossoming in the desert. But often they say only "a community will be built here." They carefully neglect to mention just who will build it.

As to insurance, older people don't buy much of the life variety, naturally, but they're prime candidates for supplemental health and hospitalization policies. Some agents target the old, and there have been instances of older people purchasing multiple policies, obligating themselves for annual premiums in excess of income. Older people, especially those who are lonely, constitute easy marks for agents who call on them often, make them the center of attention as they dangle freedom from worry before their eyes, while they butter them up to sign policies that will prove worthless to them, or at best with premiums amounting to more than they can afford.

The dodge on the home heating system beyond repair and in immediate need of replacement is well known. Representatives of fly-by-night outfits frequently make the rounds, victimizing older people especially. And there exists no record that any one of these agents *ever* found a furnace whose condition was, at best, anything but near hopeless. Outfits selling roofing and complete rewiring jobs frequently follow similar tactics. Many are the rueful older persons and couples taken in on these items.

None of this *needs* to happen. The cardinal rule is: don't trust any salesperson with tricky spiels, with or without lovely four-color brochures, suddenly appearing at your door. Before you purchase that lot alongside that sparkling lake, go take a look. *Never* buy real estate sight unseen. Transportation may seem expensive, but it's not nearly so costly as tying yourself to paying for a patch of perpetual mud, a plot without hope of ever connecting with electricity, sewer, and phone lines, a piece of desolate land in the midst of nowhere. And even if the deal appears decent, still check out the company's credentials, its track record, and insofar as possible try to determine the likelihood of the development ever amounting to any more than a land speculator's dream. You can also check with the federal Office of Interstate Land Sales, a part of the Department of Housing and Urban Development, and with an appropriate state agency. Maybe you can't predict a development's future with any certitude, but there's no need to buy a whole pig in a poke. Be skeptical, from start to finish. If you don't buy, at worst you'll hurt a salesperson's feelings. But if you purchase a lemon, you can bring yourself to near ruin.

Be especially careful with health insurance. Read the policy's fine print, or have someone you can trust read it for you. If necessary, take it to a lawyer. All these policies have some kind of limitations, exclusions, and deductibles of one type or another; some pay little or nothing if you have another policy; and some pay off only under the most stringent circumstances. And cast an especially flinty eye on the price.

A policy that costs "only pennies" has a way of adding many dollars to your regular financial obligations, or it might return you "only pennies" in benefits. Then, after you've absorbed all this, still put off a decision. Think it over and, again, consult someone you trust. If nothing else, consult your state insurance regulatory agency to find out about the company's reputation and payoff record—and certainly if you've a complaint let that agency know.

Don't be flattered because a salesperson pays you all that attention. He or she is not there to keep you company, but solely to earn a commission. Remember, it's your money, and if you're going to shell it out, see that you're getting a product of some value to *you*.

You don't need to depend on some unknown company representative to determine the condition of your furnace, roofing, and so on. Your local gas, electric, or oil company will check out your furnace at little or no cost and give you the truth—if for no other reason than they're selling fuel, not appliances, and have nothing to gain or lose. If you want to know about your roof or your electrical system (and certainly these, like the furnace, should be checked regularly), have a local dealer or reputable craftsman look things over. This might cost a little, but not much, and surely less than an item you don't need.

Today numerous groups and government agencies exist for consumer protection. And on the whole they do a good job. But your best protection remains simply this: caveat emptor— let the buyer beware. Be especially wary of glittering promises, free lunches, and costs amounting to "only a few cents." As the cynical old editor told the fledgling reporter: "If your mother says she loves you, check it out."

Getting ripped off is no condition of being older, or of being any age. You don't *have* to let the leeches feed on you.

LIE #28

It's bad to dwell on the past

More than anything else, this attitude is a product of a future-oriented society. It stems from historically characteristic American optimism: there's something better over the next hill, the future will be better. Settlement eventually closed out the geographic frontier, but there remained plenty of other frontiers to be optimistic about.

And the idea that the future will be better has worked out in a sufficient number of cases to give it validity— at least in the eyes of most Americans. How many people, as I do, know of someone who concluded during the Great Depression that the future had been forever closed, that times would never get better, only to wind up affluent in the 1950s?

Looking ever forward comes naturally to children, of course; where else might they fix their eyes? They're encouraged to think in terms of time to come, and to defer a number of rewards and gratifications.

Although what's normal for children is not necessarily so for older people, few older people actually stop looking ahead—additional retirement years, the next holiday or birthday, and so on. But that doesn't mean that we can't consider the past too, at least now and then. Who among us doesn't like to reminisce, to recall cherished moments of some time ago? And what could possibly be wrong with that!

True, there are those who concen-trate entirely on bygone years to the exclusion or near exclusion of both present and future. But these people at least border on the pathological. There are others, mostly grumpy persons, who constantly yearn for the "good old days," even though when pinned down they really can't think of a lot of things good about them.

Most of us are normal, and there's nothing abnormal about recalling childhood, youth, and other times, savoring memories and talking about them. And as they grow older, your children are delighted to hear more about your past, for it helps give them a feeling of continuity.

Your past is all yours, after all, no one else's. So enjoy recalling it whenever you wish, without fear of being considered dotty for the exercise.

LIE #29

Old people die because they're old

Not so.

Dr. Hans Selye has said flatly, and other physicians agree, "Nobody ever died of old age." Disease, accident, body abuse, what have you, but not old age.

And yet we continue to think of age as a cause of death. Actually, if we say someone died because he or she was very old, we might as well say someone was born because he or she was very young.

I was five when I first viewed the remains of someone I had known. He was a house painter who had lived four doors from my grandmother's house in Lima, Ohio. I had watched him at work. I asked my grandmother why he had died, and I remember her answering, "Oh, he was very old."

Over the years I've come to see how wrong such a response is.

It's true that the older one becomes, the less statistical life expectancy that person can enjoy. But everyone at any age has an even chance of reaching his or her life expectancy. For example, if you had a life expectancy at first of seventy years, when and if you reach that age you then have a life expectancy of eighty-one. At age one hundred it's one hundred one. But at any rate the statistical chance of reaching the expectancy figure is fifty-fifty. So everyone who dies falls short of his or her expectancy figure and does not, you might well say, become old enough.

From this point of view, old age is hardly a cause of death. On the contrary, it stands as a symbol of victory over all forces of destruction, decay, and dissolution that threaten us throughout life.

An older person should be seen as a human being who escaped becoming an infant-mortality statistic, a victim of a fatal childhood disease, an accident in midlife, lowered resistance and disorders of later life. He or she actually is a triumph, a living symbol of vitality and good fortune, and perhaps prudent living.

We all die. But none of us falls victim to old age.

LIE #30

People are what they are, so it's useless to try to change attitudes toward the older

So you can't change human nature. The trouble is, we don't know where human nature leaves off and environment begins. We do know that we can change environment (we've been doing it since humans first appeared on earth), and we also know that a changed environment frequently breeds changed attitudes.

And nature itself, human or otherwise, can take some strange twists. In all forms of life, survival is a strong drive. Yet it is sometimes overridden by other drives. For example, a bee dies when it stings, but still it stings. A female spider devours the male after mating, but that doesn't curb the male's sex drive. Some members of ant colonies are soldiers. Their sole function is to ward off enemies regardless of survival. In many forms of life there are motivations serving the colony's or the community's, not the individual's, survival.

In humans there are numerous drives either not related or only tangentially related to survival: levels of personal gratification and enjoyment, acquisitiveness, greed, desire for power, and the more praiseworthy qualities of empathy, knowledge seeking, capacity to love, and so on. And we're wrong to attach the tag "human nature" to these, for they are simply reflections of values—often contradictory—society upholds. After all, we know that some societies are not acquisitive, some are not aggressive, some find the term "private property" meaningless.

Given sufficiently strong motivation, cultural outlooks and habits can be changed. Take one small example, from Arthur Clarke. He tells of a people in Africa among whom adult males, for a time longer than tribal memory, had worn a bone through the lower central cartilage of the nose. Missionaries had tried to get that people to abandon this defacing practice and had finally given up. Then the Polaroid camera came along. Every member of the group acquired or borrowed one.

But you can't focus a Polaroid camera with a bone in your nose. Within a few months the nose-bones disappeared. This would seem to indicate that even the most stubborn social practices are changeable if there exists sufficient motivation to alter them.

So with our attitudes toward old in America. What would it take to wake us up to the desirability of a decent approach to them? I believe that the motivation lies in realizing who the aging are. And they are *us,* all of us. Shortchange the old today, and you shortchange yourself tomorrow. There lies the nub of it.

Yes, we might have to lay out more money to help those millions of Americans experiencing or soon to face rather bleak years of older age. No one knows how much, but we can afford it. Right now the United States spends only about 5 percent of a gross national product of more than a trillion dollars on aid to older people. On the other hand Americans shell out more than eleven billion dollars annually on tobacco and alcohol, and the defense budget has long since passed one hundred billion a year. Usually what we can't afford is that which we don't want to afford. It's a matter of priorities, and I think ours are overdue for change.

Most of all, we must say to ourselves, "Hey, those guys are human too. And there in a few years go us."

I would hope that with this book I might stimulate at least a modest change in attitudes toward the old. If so, I'll have done my bit toward demolishing Lie #30.

Epilogue

What is an old person?

I remember before my parents were forty Walter Pitkin published his book *Life Begins at Forty,* and since they were interested in it I wondered how they could subscribe to such a preposterous idea. How could life begin when it was shortly to end? I wondered how they would hold up after crossing that awful age barrier. I knew that my two living grandparents had to be over forty, but in that distant sunset land beyond forty, one age seemed pretty much the same as another. Forty, sixty, eighty—all equally old.

Contrast this with a more recent attitude.

Not long ago I sat beside Lowell Thomas on a television interview. Thomas began network newscasting when the now-retired Eric Sevareid was thirteen years old. His television program "Lowell Thomas Remembers" is widely seen on the Public Broadcasting System. He had recently remarried after the death of Fran, his wife of fifty-eight years. He went skiing on his honeymoon trip, which covered seventy thousand miles, during which he celebrated his eighty-fifth birthday.

I found as I stared at him (yes, stared) that I couldn't regard Lowell Thomas as more than middle aged. I tried to detect something about him in the framework of my conception and definition of "aged," and I failed. His face was somewhat weather-beaten and craggy, but it had been exposed to a lot of weather, and I have seen such faces on much younger men. He limped slightly, due to a horse accident that pulverized a hip some thirty years earlier.

Granted, Lowell Thomas is somewhat an exception. For every vigorous man of his age, though, we can easily find a much younger person who is worn out or decrepit. What then *is* old?

I have come to the conclusion that when we speak of old age we really don't know what we're talking about. There is no neat, airtight definition. But there are numerous other kinds.

One is "post-retirement" age, beginning at an arbitrary sixty-five, which Germany's Chancellor Otto von Bismarck set at a time when relatively few workers lived beyond that. In Russia the retirement age for men is sixty. Now in the United States the age is moving from sixty-five to seventy. Some people would do away with retirement age entirely. In any case, retirement age indicates a certain number of calendar years of life. It doesn't tell us much about old.

On the basis of life expectancy for males in the United States, dividing life into three equal periods—youth, middle age, and aged—we can calculate middle age at from 23⅓ to 46⅔ years. Any male forty-seven or older then is aged. On the life-expectancy basis, middle age for women begins at twenty-five. All this, of course, is too silly to consider.

No one denies that we are mortal. Each of us will one day die. There is no escape from the eventual accident or disease from which we'll not recover. When this occurs early in life, the blow must be very forceful to overwhelm the organism's integrity, attacking a single organ or system or, in the case of severe accident, the entire body. If this occurs in later years, when resistance is lower and integrity more easily breeched, the blow need not be so powerful.

So what, then, about the ability to withstand such an attack as a measure of old? Unfortunately for purposes of definition, the rate of what one might call deterioration varies greatly among individuals. It's not a useful measurement.

Gerontologists have now taken to dividing old age into the young-old—sixty-five to seventy-four—and the old-old—seventy-five and up. This again is purely arbitrary, but perhaps useful.

Are we then to consider Lowell Thomas among the old-old? Yes. And once we get over equating age with decrepitude, we'll find that the only meaningful definition of age will be arithmetical.

And old is beautiful. A person with many years behind, far from being a symbol of disaster, represents instead victory over the forces out to kill us in our cribs, on the streets, and among the microscopic life and pollution in the air, water, and food we take in every day. And when we finally adopt the idea that old is beautiful, perhaps we'll drop the euphemisms "elderly," "senior citizen," and so on. We might say "old" in the way we now say "tall" or "great." And we might even try regarding human life—especially our own—as we regard a meal. This "life is a banquet" idea I find an interesting analogy.

Enjoying a meal can be divided into three main parts: anticipation, participation, and satisfaction.

At the outset we bring appetite, which is said to be the best sauce. An appetizer of some sort is the first course, but we are still hungry and expect to enjoy the whole meal. We then proceed to the entree, the dishes accompanying it, and finally to dessert. All this is participation. Finally, over coffee, we bask in the satisfaction of having eaten.

We would be out of whack if we didn't enjoy each stage in turn. If, for example, during the anticipation stage we were unhappy that we weren't yet attacking the main course, we might seem maladjusted. And so we would if during the satisfaction stage we bemoaned the fact that we were not still hungry and eating. Some ancient Romans were out of adjustment in this way. When sated, they would leave the banquet for the vomitorium, rid themselves of what they had consumed, and return for more.

Our culture, I believe, approaches the life span in a similarly maladjusted manner. We are brought up to believe that the middle of life is the substance of all living; that childhood is a limited, not-quite-human condition; and that old age is a crime. Some of this comes from our twisted sense of usefulness. Children and old people are not as "useful" as middle-aged adults. Certainly they are not—or at least are not allowed to be—as economically productive. We hold children back, and we shunt the old aside—out of sight, we hope—into retirement. But even granting the somewhat shaky economic argument for keeping children and removing the older from the work force, we still have categories of usefulness, particularly for the older, that can be highly valuable.

Let's face it, there's more than a hint of ice-floe ethics in our attitude toward the old. When elderly Eskimos could no longer hunt, or even sew skins or build shelters, obliging the society their relatives placed them on ice floes or otherwise exposed them to extinction so as not to diminish the food supply needlessly. Cruel as this may seem, it had community survival value. But when a society becomes industrialized, when one farmer can feed many people, the practice becomes anachronistic. Still, we insist on placing older people as a *group* on the ice floes of retirement or "rest" homes or loneliness, or otherwise expose them. This all reflects prejudice, not survival value.

Only recently have we seen the awakening of more serious and humane attitudes toward older people—in the number of organizations working to redress wrongs, in the way older people are organizing themselves, and in mass-media campaigns to call attention to some special aspect of old. We still, however, have a long way to go.

Every stage of life has its limitations. Jean Kerr once related that when one of their children asked, "*Why* do I have to do it?" she and her husband responded, "Because it's our house and we are bigger than you." Midlife has its limitations too. The need to provide a livelihood for self and others hems one in. Even though the job be less than satisfactory, we must have it; there's no other means of survival. Only the brave—or the reckless—in middle age dare "do their own thing."

The final stage of life is not without limitations either. But as I've been at pains to point out, most of them are socially concocted, not at all intrinsic. Older people show a gradual decline in physical strength and flexibility and in the speed of some mental processes.

Sexual fires burn not as brightly, although they by no means need to die out. Older people show an increasing erosion of organic integrity—that is, the ability of organs and systems to ward off disease and to function in harmony with each other. (I'm not talking here about malfunction; that can occur at any age.) That's about it. All other limitations are socially—and needlessly—imposed.

If we believe that society, or the community or state, is the important entity, then we believe that the individual must be subordinate in every respect to the group, and there is no point in trying to do anything for an individual beyond discouraging mutiny. If, however, we believe states and communities exist for the purpose of making each individual's life better, then efforts to encourage independence and to enhance the quality of living and alleviate injustice and suffering are certainly justifiable and worthwhile.

Let us imagine a society whose citizens are encouraged to regard time in a less linear fashion, and in which there are no prejudices toward the old. Here an old person will enjoy respect for having made his or her contribution, whatever it is. He or she will enjoy satisfaction, offer advice, and be welcomed to work or allowed to stop. Destitution will be absent. Whatever his or her financial status, the older person will not lack creature comforts, or medical help, or delights of the mind. If infirmity comes, the limitations will be offset to the extent medicine and technology make this possible, and the extent the productive segment of society will wish or can afford to do this will be greater than at present in the United States.

Doctors will not be prejudiced against the older, and advertising will have outgrown Pepsi-generation mentality—indeed, by the time the Pepsi generation has matured, gray will be beautiful. Sex will be enjoyed without disapproval, and comfort and dignity will be more readily available. Older people's loss of strength and flexibility will be offset by personal environments that will amplify power and mobility and aid failing senses. Above all, the wishes of the *individual* will govern efforts to "care" for him or her.

Millennial thinking? Perhaps. But even a few small steps toward the goal will enhance the chances of all of us to live with satisfaction until we die.

And the lies will vanish.